Do T
Storytelling for You and Your Students

Annie Weissman

Linworth
PUBLISHING, INC

Linworth Publishing, Inc.
Worthington, Ohio 43085

M000247957

DEDICATION

For all my children who loved to listen to stories: Emily, Elizabeth, Nick, Eric, and Vanessa.

ACKNOWLEDGEMENTS

Thanks to Susan Bailyn for allowing me to use the flannelboard patterns she drew, and to Susan Garvin, who helped me with the math.

Library of Congress Cataloging-in-Publication Data

Weissman, Annie, 1948–

    Do tell! : storytelling for you and your students / Annie Weissman.

        p. cm.

    Includes bibliographical references (p.) and index.

    ISBN 1-58683-074-0 (perfectbound)

    1. Storytelling.   I. Title

LB1042.W47 2002

372.67'7--dc21   2002032969

Published by Linworth Publishing, Inc.

480 East Wilson Bridge Road, Suite L

Worthington, Ohio 43085

ISBN: 1-58683-074-0

5 4 3 2 1

Table of Contents

Introduction

I have been telling stories for more than 30 years. I've been teaching others how to tell stories for almost as long. When I first started to teach storytelling, I'd lecture and tell stories. When I ran into participants six months or a year later, I'd ask how the storytelling was going. Most of the time the answer was, "Well, I haven't tried it yet, but I so enjoyed your workshop." Struck by the fact that the participants had never made the leap to doing their own storytelling, I started to give workshops where the participants were required to tell short stories. When I met these participants later, they all reported they told the stories they learned in the workshop. Some had even learned new ones. Many expressed problems finding stories that were easy to learn and tell.

The purpose of this book is to get you into storytelling, to provide you with resources to increase your repertoire, to provide a curriculum that fits in the school library program, and to suggest ideas to get students telling stories, too. All of the stories in this book are drawn from traditional folk literature.

The intended audience of this book is teacher-librarians of all levels, but this book can also be used by teachers, youth group leaders, teachers of children's literature, and religious-school teachers.

It is a book for beginners. This book will explain how to tell stories, as well as provide the source material of short and easy-to-learn stories.

Do Tell! Storytelling for You and Your Students will teach you how to select an easy story for telling and how to learn the story. It contains specific lesson plans for a unit in which students learn to tell stories, as well as a time line, strategies, suggestions, and ideas for holding a storytelling festival at your school.

The first part of the book concerns how and why to tell stories and includes lesson plans for incorporating storytelling into the library. Bibliographies are included in each chapter. The second part of the book provides stories to tell.

Chapter 1 reviews the literature for purposes and advantages of storytelling. These are then directly related to state and national academic standards as well as standardized test objectives. These are the fodder for objectives and rationale for lesson plans.

Chapter 2 is about how to begin. It has criteria for the selection of stories as well as hints for how to learn a story. There is a bibliography of books with short stories for beginning storytellers.

Chapter 3 gives information and tips on presenting stories. This includes the use of your voice and body in telling the story; setting up the best conditions, such as room arrangement; student behavioral expectations; and stylized beginnings.

Chapter 4 shows how to use proverbs as a step to storytelling and to becoming comfortable speaking in front of a group.

The integration of storytelling into the library (and classroom) curriculum is discussed in Chapter 5. There are sample programs that relate to many areas of the curriculum.

Board storytelling is introduced in Chapter 6. It includes information about the differences between traditional and board storytelling, tips and resources for making flannelboard stories, and instructions for how to effectively present board stories. Two board-story patterns are included.

Chapter 7 covers the curriculum unit for student storytelling. The lessons start with board storytelling and proceed to traditional storytelling.

Chapter 8 explains how to conduct school and district-wide storytelling festivals. Specific ideas for how to organize a storytelling festival are contained in this chapter.

Chapter 9 contains stories for the beginning storyteller. I have retold these stories from folk literature, all of which are in the public domain. Storytellers would call these versions "bare bones," into which each storyteller breathes more life. They are put in order of ease to tell, "A" being the easiest and "C" being a bit more challenging.

After Chapter 9 there is a bibliography of books about storytelling and a list of Web sites. These are for those readers who want to expand their background knowledge of storytelling.

At the end of the book is an alphabetical title index for the stories included in this book.

Chapter 1 What is Storytelling? Why Do It?

This book is not intended for scholars or folklorists. It is for the teacher-librarians and teachers who want a special way to connect with students and parents. A story is a gift.

It's okay to be a beginning storyteller with children. They will appreciate the time, effort, and guts that go into the preparation and telling. Children need to know that everything doesn't come easily to everyone. The story doesn't have to be perfect if it's from the heart. Listeners can tell when there's sincerity behind the story.

THE POWER OF STORYTELLING

Storytelling is an ancient oral art form. It is telling a story directly to listeners, without the use of a book or props. Before the written word, it was the way that people communicated across generations. It brings people together for a shared experience. Storytelling is accessible to everyone who speaks the same language. It is entertainment as well as a window into the human condition and problem solving. A warm, non-authoritarian bond is formed between the teller and the listener. The teller needs the listeners as much as the listeners enjoy the teller's stories.

Third-grade teacher Gregory Denman, in his essay "Daring to Tell: The Making of a Storyteller" in *Tales as Tools: The Power of Storytelling in the Classroom,* writes convincingly about the difference between reading a story and telling it. When he reads a story aloud, he feels tied to the print. When he tells a story, his version can be as free as his unfettered hands (4).

Bill Harley, in his essay "Playing with the Wall" in *Who Says?,* writes that "a story's success depends upon the intimacy created between the teller and listener" (130). During a powerful and well-told story, the listener feels that the story is being told only to him or her. The images stay in the listeners' minds. My own experience bears this out. For two years early in my career, I was a children's librarian with the Phoenix Public Library. For part of my job, I visited local schools and told stories to entice students to visit the public library branch during the summer. Ten years later, walking in a midtown shopping mall, a young adult in his twenties stopped me and asked if I remembered him. He went on to say that I had visited his school and told a story that had knocked him out of his seat. Upon further questioning, I realized that it was my telling of "The Golden Arm" that he remembered so vividly. This is not an isolated experience. Over the past twenty-five years, many people have stopped me and asked if I remembered telling them a specific story, such as "the one about the girl and the giant" ("Molly Whuppie and the Double-Faced Giant") and "the one about the crab's eyes" ("The Crab and the Jaguar," available in my book *Transforming Storytimes into Reading and Writing Lessons* (Linworth, 2001)).

Scholars believe that fairy tales have psychological importance for children. For instance, the giants in fairy tales are the incarnation of adults (Bettleheim 7). "Hansel and Gretel" is all about separation anxiety. The people in folk and fairy tales are often the embodiment of basic human characteristics: jealousy, greed, honesty, and so on. Folk literature lays bare the never changing universal truths (Bettleheim 159).

Joseph Sobol, in the essay "Innervision and Innertext" in *Who Says?,* delineates the difference between the oral and written cultures. He states that the oral culture depends on the ear, has warmth, employs feelings, has a sense of immediacy, touches the interior of people, is natural, and promotes a language of synthesis. He states that the written culture relies on the eye; promotes individualism, detachment, and logical and analytical thinking; and is separated from nature (202).

"Oral storytelling has the uncanny power of allowing us to enter the imagination," Rafe Martin says in his essay "Between Teller and Listener" in *Who Says?* (142). He goes on to write that in storytelling, all the scenes, characters, and events must be communicated by the voice, language, body, and emotion of the storyteller. There is an equality between the listener and teller, as the skills of both are needed for the story to work. The audience must be there for the telling to happen. Listeners respond to the story and the way it's told. They must be active listeners who are willing to participate. Listeners want to be taken out of the ordinary world. They want their humanity touched, their hearts moved, their funny bones tickled, and their intellect engaged.

GOOD REASONS TO TELL STORIES

The reasons to tell stories are many. Listening to and telling a story gives both the teller and the listener a sense of belonging. Storytelling gives students practice in listening and imagining. It makes students more sensitive to other cultures. It gives students a deeper understanding of who they are. It is a shared and powerful experience. Storytelling addresses the needs of aural learners and students who do not have good reading skills, allowing them to fully participate. It allows nonreaders of all abilities to enjoy literature.

Storytelling preserves the oral tradition and passes on the beliefs and values of a culture. It enables listeners and tellers to better compose their own stories by revealing the patterns of story plots and characters. Storytelling helps children delight in language and widen their vocabulary, and it acquaints them with word styles and rhythms. Students can be tempted to delve further into all areas of the curriculum with storytelling as it exposes them to new ideas and concepts. It inspires children to read different types of literature and to become storytellers and writers. It increases vocabulary by exposing children to meanings of unfamiliar words in context.

Many teacher-librarians use storytelling as a lure into the library and books. Their goals are to have students associate the library with enjoyment and make them lifelong learners.

Melissa A. Heckler, in "Two Traditions" in *Who Says?*, states that stories tell us "we are all different, unique, and yet bound together in similar needs for love, support, and recognition, which we receive only in proportion to our relatedness to others in the human community" (31).

Rebecca Isbell and Shirley C. Raines state, "Because children are more involved in creating the pictures of the story, they are more likely to remember the characters, the sequence, and the moral of the story" (8). By listening to stories, children can understand the consequences of actions and choices without having to physically experience them.

STANDARDS-BASED INSTRUCTION

For storytellers in an educational setting, it is imperative to be able to pinpoint how storytelling will contribute to students' competencies and to know which standards storytelling addresses.

The national language arts standards, as articulated by the National Council of Teachers of English (NCTE) and the International Reading Association (IRA), are available on the Internet. Standard 12 relates directly to storytelling. It states, "Students use spoken, written, and visual language to accomplish their own purposes." More specific standards can be found for most states on the Web site for the state's department of education. Two examples follow.

Most state standards have listening skills as a requirement. The Arizona Department of Education's Web site states Language Arts Standard 3 (Listening and Speaking) as: "Students effectively listen and speak in situations that serve different purposes and involve a variety of audiences." For Grades 1–3, the standard includes telling a story. In Grades 9–12, the same standard means being able to "deliver oral interpretations of literary or original works." The performance objectives for the Arizona standards include the requirement that students be able to listen to stories and anticipate patterns in familiar stories.

New York has a similar requirement. The New York State Education Department's Web site gives English Language Arts Standard 2 as: "Students will read, write, listen, and speak for literary response and expression. Students will read and listen to oral, written, and electronically produced texts and performances ... "

It is important to determine the state and local standards that apply to storytelling so the objectives can be incorporated into lesson plans. This ensures that storytelling is seen as part of the academic program.

Valerie Marsh, in Chapter 1 of *Storyteller's Sampler*, states that there are specific skills that can be taught to students via storytelling. They are:

- Developing the higher-level thinking skills of sequencing, critical thinking, short- and long-term memory, analysis, and synthesis
- Gaining a general knowledge base
- Gaining an understanding of other cultures
- Developing creative imagination

Teacher-librarians do not have to be polished storytellers. This book is not intended for those who seek to perform and make storytelling a career. Teacher-librarians are in a unique position to tell the same story many times, to different classes. Storytelling can enhance any program and make it more fun for both the teacher-librarian and the students. Chapter 7 has specific lesson plans to integrate storytelling into social studies, reading, math, and the writing process.

Many standardized tests have listening portions as well as questions that cover the reading skills, such as sequencing events in a story. Listening skills can be enhanced by storytelling.

Listening to someone tell stories is an enjoyable way to practice these skills, including the skills needed to understand oral directions for taking a test.

Bibliography

Arizona Department of Education. "Standard 3: Listening and Speaking." *Language Arts Standards.* 12 Sept. 2002 <http://www.ade.az.gov/standards/language-arts/std3.pdf>.

Baker, Augusta, and Ellin Greene. *Storytelling Art & Technique.* New York: Bowker, 1987.

Bettleheim, Bruno. *Uses of Enchantment: The Meaning and Importance of Fairy Tales.* New York: Knopf, 1976.

Birch, Carol L., and Melissa A. Heckler. *Who Says? Essays on Pivotal Issues in Contemporary Storytelling.* Little Rock, AR: August, 1996.

Denman, Gregory. "Daring to Tell: The Making of a Storyteller." *Tales as Tools: The Power of Storytelling in the Classroom.* Jonesboro, TN: National Storytelling, 1994. (2–4).

Harley, Bill. "Playing with the Wall." *Who Says? Essays on Pivotal Issues in Contemporary Storytelling.* Ed. Carol L. Birch and Melissa A. Heckler. Little Rock, AR: August, 1996. (129–140).

Heckler, Melissa A. "Two Traditions." *Who Says? Essays on Pivotal Issues in Contemporary Storytelling.* Ed. Carol L. Birch and Melissa A. Heckler. Little Rock, AR: August, 1996. (9–14).

Isbell, Rebecca, and Shirley C. Raines. *Tell-It-Again! 2: Easy-To-Tell Stories with Activities for Young Children.* Beltsville, MD: Gryphon, 2000. (203).

Livo, Norma J., and Sandra A. Reitz. *Storytelling: Process and Practice.* Englewood, CO: Libraries Unlimited, 1986.

Marsh, Valerie. *Storyteller's Sampler.* Fort Atkinson, WI: Alleyside, 1996.

Martin, Rafe. "Between Teller and Listener." "Between Teller and Listener: The Reciprocity of Storytelling." *Who Says? Essays on Pivotal Issues in Contemporary Storytelling.* Ed. Carol L. Birch and Melissa A. Heckler. Little Rock, AR: August, 1996. (141–154).

National Council of Teachers of English and International Reading Association. *Standards for the English Language Arts.* 12 Sept. 2002 <http://www.ncte.org/standards/standards.shtml>.

National Storytelling Association. *Tales as Tools: The Power of Story in the Classroom.* Jonesboro, TN: National Storytelling, 1994.

New York State Education Department. *English Language Arts Standards.* 12 Sept. 2002 <http://www.emsc.nysed.gov/ciai/ela/elastandards/elamap.html>.

Sobol, Joseph. "Innervision and Innertext." *Who Says? Essays on Pivotal Issues in Contemporary Storytelling.* Ed. Carol L. Birch and Melissa A. Heckler. Little Rock, AR: August, 1994. (198–222).

Weissman, Annie. *Transforming Storytimes into Reading and Writing Lessons.* Worthington, OH: Linworth, 2001.

Chapter 2 Getting Started

There are many books on storytelling. The grandmother of them all is Marie Shedlock's The Art of the Storyteller. *Much of the advice in other books about storytelling was first written by Ms. Shedlock. Many books on storytelling, including* The Art of the Storyteller, *assume that the readers will be making storytelling their passion. They give advice about how to select and learn stories from the viewpoint of the longer, involved stories.*

CRITERIA FOR SELECTION OF A STORY TO TELL

There are two overriding criteria for beginning storytellers when choosing a story to learn. First, **you must love the story.** You will be putting time and effort into learning and telling the story. I guarantee you'll be telling it many times for many years. Second, the story **must be short and easy enough to master fairly quickly.** One of the biggest mistakes beginning storytellers make is to choose more story than they can comfortably learn and perform. Build up your repertoire with many short and easy stories. There is always time later to get fancy without getting discouraged. For beginning storytellers, it's important to limit the number of characters and events. Make sure the story is strong in action and has a simple plot.

The elements to look for in a good story for beginning tellers include:

- Conditions with which children are familiar
- Action (but not too gruesome)
- Repetition of words, phrases, or events
- An easy-to-follow sequence
- Interesting characters
- Predictable and cumulative events
- Humorous twists
- A structure with a brief introduction, a direct development of events in sequential order, a climax, and a brief but satisfying ending
- Not too much description or digression
- Strong, simple, powerful, rhythmic language
- A single theme which is clear and positive
- A universal subject
- A length that is short

Stories will not have all of these criteria, but look for stories that include many of them. Remember to keep in mind your limitations as a storyteller. Think about whether you are a quiet or dynamic person. Think about whether the values in the stories agree with your own. It is better to select a story that you don't have to adapt, which might change its meaning or power. Look for the best version of the story. Those versions that are "vocabulary controlled" are rarely the ones to learn. Keep in mind the curriculum and try to choose stories that relate. Since the same curriculum is taught every year, the stories can be retold to new students every year.

Who will be the audience for the story? Augusta Baker and Ellin Greene define some characteristics that my experience backs up (32). Baker and Greene's age characteristics are paired with stories that are provided in this book. Three-to-five-year-olds enjoy simple stories with rhythm and repetition, such as "Henny Penny" and "The Little Red Hen." Six-to-eight-year-olds are the best audience for traditional, straightforward folktales, such as "The Frog Prince." Nine-to-eleven-year-olds enjoy more sophisticated tales that require some reasoning and judgment, such as "Lazy Jack" and "The Golden Arm." Eleven-to-thirteen-year-olds want even more elaborate tales, tales with irony, or tales in which a deeper meaning can be inferred, such as "La Llorona" and "Pygmalion."

Multiculturalism is another aspect to consider. You may want to learn Cinderella stories from around the world to point out the universality of experience as well as the uniqueness of each culture. If you're learning "lazy" stories, choose them from several cultures so that listeners won't form a stereotype of a specific culture.

Stories cannot take the place of firsthand experiences with an ethnic group, but they can build an appreciation of cultures, traditions, and values other than our own. Stories from other cultures can prepare children to accept people of other cultures when they are encountered. Stories about a minority group foster pride and identity in the children of that group. If the stories told are representative of many groups, the universality of humans and the uniqueness of cultures can be understood and celebrated.

SOURCES FOR STORIES

Michael O. Tunnell and James S. Jacobs, in *Children's Literature, Briefly*, divide traditional fantasy into folktales; tall tales; fables; myths; and epics, ballads, and legends. The category of folktales is further divided into cumulative, porquoi (why), beast (where animals are the major characters), noodlehead, trickster, and fairy tales (which have at least one magical aspect). Many collections of folktales name the type of motifs or tales. These are helpful for the beginning storyteller who wants to tell Cinderella stories from around the world or a particular type of silly story, for example.

If stories are to be discussed as part of a character education program, consider learning fables or tales from collections such as Heather Forest's *Wisdom Tales Around the World*.

It is necessary to note that not all short stories are easy to learn. Some are complex in nature. Literary stories must be told as written, memorized word for word, and are not suggested for beginners.

A bare-bones story, usually from folklore, is one that is in the public domain. At the end of the chapter is a bibliography of books with stories suitable mostly for beginning tellers. Some of the titles in the bibliography for this chapter contain stories from specific storytellers. Their embellishment belongs to them and should be credited when the story is told. Through subsequent tellings, you embellish the story. Not all the tales are short and simple, but there are some appropriate for beginning tellers in each volume cited. Tales that I have told for more than twenty-five years are included in this book. All of them are presented "bare bones" and ready to learn.

LEARNING THE STORY

Once a story is selected, it's time to learn it. For beginners, imitation is part of the learning curve. Benjamin Franklin describes in his autobiography how he learned to write well by imitating the style of a master of writing. In the same vein, it is easier to begin telling stories that one has heard told effectively.

I recommend reading and rereading the story and reading it aloud at least twice in order to:

- Absorb the atmosphere of the story
- Visualize and feel the characters and the setting
- List or outline the sequence of events
- Decide what to memorize

There may be a chant, a repetitive phrase, specific names, a riddle, or the like. **Do not memorize the entire story!** This will be obvious to the listeners and sound artificial. Some people put the story on audiotape and listen to it while in the car, cooking, or doing other chores. Margaret Read MacDonald suggests that the audiotape of a story should be saved and played later to refresh the story if it hasn't been told for a while.

Anne Pellowski, on pages 25–28 of *The Storytelling Handbook,* asserts that there are four types of learning styles for storytellers. "Imitators" watch videotapes or audiotapes of their favorite tellers or see them in person. "Memorizers" do best by making their own recordings. "Improvisers" search for their own right words. "Picturers" use a storyboard with pictures to show the sequence of key events. It may be helpful to try each method to see what's best for you.

Practice telling the story in your own words, but refrain from using slang. Inserting slang into a folktale will produce laughs from the listeners but ruin the impact of the story. Leave out the filler words, such as *you know, okay, well then,* and *so,* that many people use in ordinary conversation.

A bare-bones story is elastic and constantly changing so that each teller can make it his or her own. After a practice, compare the story you told to the original. Was there something important that you left out?

Practice either as your own listener or with an adoring audience: your own children, pets, and so on. When you're practicing, you do not want constructive criticism. I practice stories while commuting and showering and before I go to sleep. Make sure to practice out loud.

Some storytellers suggest using a mirror, an audiotape, or videotape to practice. I am not that brave but applaud you if you can take advantage of these devices.

Bibliography of Books with Stories for Beginning Storytellers

DeSpain, Pleasant. *Tales of Nonsense and Tomfoolery.* Little Rock, AR: August, 2001.

DeSpain, Pleasant. *Tales of Tricksters.* Little Rock, AR: August, 2001.

DeSpain, Pleasant. *Tales of Wisdom and Justice.* Little Rock, AR: August, 2001.

DeSpain, Pleasant. *Thirty-Six Multicultural Tales to Tell.* Little Rock, AR: August, 1993.

Forest, Heather. *Wisdom Tales from Around the World.* Little Rock, AR: August, 1996.

Holt, David, and Bill Mooney, eds. *Ready-To-Tell Tales.* Little Rock, AR: August, 1994.

Holt, David, and Bill Mooney, eds. *Ready-To-Tell Tales from Around the World.* Little Rock, AR: August, 2000.

Isbell, Rebecca, and Shirley C. Raines. *Tell It Again! 2: Easy-To-Tell Stories with Activities for Young Children.* Beltsville, MD: Gryphon, 2000.

MacDonald, Margaret Read. *The Storytellers Start-Up Book: Finding, Learning, Performing & Using Folktales Including Twelve Tellable Tales.* Little Rock, AR: August, 1993.

MacDonald, Margaret Read. *Twenty Tellable Tales: Audience Participation Folktales for the Beginning Storyteller.* New York: Wilson, 1986.

MacDonald, Margaret Read. *When the Lights Go Out: Twenty Scary Tales to Tell.* New York: Wilson, 1988.

Marsh, Valerie. *Storyteller's Sampler.* Fort Atkinson, WI: Alleyside, 1996.

Shannon, George. *More True Lies: 18 Tales for You to Judge.* New York: Greenwillow, 2001.

Shannon, George. *Stories to Solve: Folktales from around the World.* New York: Beech Tree, 1991.

Sherman, Josepha. *Rachel the Clever and Other Jewish Folktales.* Little Rock, AR: August, 1993.

Sierra, Judy, and Robert Kaminski. *Multicultural Folktales: Stories to Tell Young Children.* Phoenix, AZ: Oryx, 1991.

Warren, Jean. *"Cut & Tell" Scissor Stories for Winter.* Everett, WA: Warren, 1984.

Young, Richard, and Judy Dockrey Young. *Favorite Scary Stories of American Children: 23 Tales for Ages 5 to 10.* Little Rock, AR: August, 1990.

Bibliography of Books Cited in This Chapter

Baker, Augusta, and Ellin Greene. *Storytelling Art & Technique.* New York: Bowker, 1987.

Forest, Heather. *Wisdom Tales Around the World.* Little Rock, AR: August, 1996.

MacDonald, Margaret Read. *The Storytellers Start-Up Book: Finding, Learning, Performing & Using Folktales Including Twelve Tellable Tales.* Little Rock, AR: August, 1993.

Pellowski, Anne. *The Storytelling Handbook.* New York: Simon, 1995.

Shedlock, Marie L. *The Art of the Storyteller.* 1915. New York: Dover, 1951.

Tunnell, Michael O., and James S. Jacobs. *Children's Literature, Briefly.* Upper Saddle River, NJ: Merrill, 2000.

Weissman, Annie. *Transforming Storytimes into Reading and Writing Lessons.* Worthington, OH: Linworth, 2001.

Chapter 3 Presenting a Story

PERSONAL PRESENTATION

The posture and stance of the storyteller are important cues for the listeners. I almost always stand when telling a story. Standing allows free movement, total supervision of the audience, and visibility to the audience.

The voice and body are used together to put the story across to the listeners. Mumbling is forbidden. Diction must be clear so the listeners can understand the words. The story must be told expressively but not overly so. It's not acting; it's storytelling. Padraic Colum, in *Story Telling, Old and New,* gives sage advice: "The storyteller has to relate the happenings as if he or she had just discovered them as something going on" (9).

VOICE

The volume of your voice should be loud enough for all listeners to hear comfortably without straining. Your voice needs to be projected from the diaphragm, not shouted. Volume can also be used for emphasis. While telling "In the Dark, Dark Woods," my voice is soft until the end when I shout, "a MONSTER!" Almost every child will experience that thrilling chill of scariness. The scare is momentary. Children laugh afterwards and want to learn how to tell the story to their older brothers and sisters, so they can scare them.

Your voice can also be used to control a restless or misbehaving child. Simply directing the telling and your eye contact at such a child is often enough to bring him or her back into the story.

PACE

The pace of speaking should be changed to match what's happening in the story. A great story can be ruined by being told too quickly for listeners to grasp the words or so slowly that listeners are impatient for the words.

PITCH

The pitch of your voice should be comfortable for you and the listeners. If you have a voice that is high in pitch, try telling a story in the lower ranges of your pitch. High pitched voices are difficult to listen to for an extended period. The pitch of your voice can also be used to tell the story. You can choose to change the pitch or tone for different characters in the story. When you're a beginner, beware of trying too many different voices in one story. It's easy to get confused and start using the wolf's voice for the grandmother's.

PAUSES

There are several uses for pausing during a story. A pause in the middle of a sentence lends emphasis to those words to come. For instance, while telling "The Teeny Tiny Woman," I pause after the words "bone" and "grave" in the sentence "The teeny tiny woman took the teeny tiny **bone** from the teeny tiny **grave** and put it in her teeny tiny pocket." This sets up the suspense around the bone and the voice from the cupboard.

DIALECTS

A word of caution about dialects: don't use one unless it's your ethnic background. This may seem too politically correct, but I have cringed when I've heard storytellers do stereotyped Mexican accents. Listeners will not enjoy an attempted but bungled accent. One way to tell a story effectively is to listen to a native speaker's pace and phrasing, and incorporate them into the telling.

FACIAL EXPRESSIONS

Facial expressions are an important part of storytelling, but they should not be so exaggerated as to cartoon or overtake the story. Use them to portray a character or an emotion. Try them out in a mirror to make sure they ring true to the story and its characters.

SOUND EFFECTS

Sound effects can be effective if used sparingly. In "The Golden Arm," one of the stories in this book, it is fun to use sound effects for the knocking at the door, the wind howling through the trees, and the footsteps on the stairs. Problems occur when sound effects are used as cheap tricks. Then they take away from, rather than enhance, the story.

GESTURES

Gestures can also enhance a story. Hands can be used to indicate movement (for example, putting something in a pocket), an object, or the greatness or smallness of a person or an object. If the audience doesn't know what your body is trying to tell, then the gestures are distractions rather than enhancements. Avoid overuse of hand gestures as it diverts the audience's attention. Also check the mirror for annoying mannerisms like twirling a lock of hair, touching your face, or tugging on a sleeve.

EYE CONTACT

Eye contact is very important. Each listener should feel the story is being told to him or her directly. Make sure to make eye contact with all of the listeners during the telling of a story. Strong eye contact is also an effective way of silencing talkers and getting children to keep their hands to themselves.

RHETORICAL QUESTIONS

Refrain from rhetorical questions. Many times listeners will attempt to answer the questions. This can break the story spell.

CONFIDENCE AND SINCERITY

Storytellers need to project confidence in the story and sincerity in its telling. This is where the selection and preparation of the story figure into the presentation. If you truly like the story you're presenting, you will come across as sincere. If you have practiced sufficiently, you will come across as confident. A trick to calm nervousness is to breathe in and out slowly and deeply and tense and relax your toes.

Some storytellers are dramatic while others are restrained. Make sure to match your story and style with the telling. All the beginning stories in this book, although written, are meant to be told in a conversational style.

SETTING UP THE PLACE

Try to have as much control as possible over the setting of the storytelling. If it's in your own library, set it up for optimal visibility. It's best to be able to see all the listeners without turning your head. A third of a circle is best, with rows as needed. Circular seating is a nightmare as your back is always towards members of the audience. If students are seated in straight rows, it's better to have more rows of fewer students. If you have many students in one row, you have to turn your head too far to see each end of the row.

Set the storytelling area out of the main flow of the library to decrease interruptions and distractions. The picture book shelves can be arranged to form two or three sides of a private area. Remember to seat students so the audience is facing the books, not the main area of the library.

Rules for storytime should be made clear before any storytelling begins. Insist on absolute silence. Let students know they may ask questions *after* the story, not during.

SETTING THE MOOD

Some storytellers begin with a "ritual." Rituals can be taught to students and used to set the mood. Short poems that accompany the lighting of a candle are traditional. I remember the story candle from my own childhood when I attended story hour at the Teaneck Public Library in Teaneck, New Jersey. At the end of the story hour, we children made a wish while the storyteller blew out the candle.

Ritual openings come from all over the world. I heard Diane Wolkstein, a storyteller from New York City, begin with a Haitian ritual. The storyteller says, "cric." If the listeners want to hear that storyteller relate a story, they loudly say, "CRAC!"

Norma J. Livo and Sandra A. Reitz report other ritual openings (6). The Sudanese one goes like this:

> Storyteller: I'm going to tell a story.
> Audience: Right!
> Storyteller: It's a lie!
> Audience: Right!
> Storyteller: But not everything in it is false.
> Audience: Right!

As for endings, sometimes the best way to end the story is, "And that's the story of —."

AUDIENCE PARTICIPATION

Before presenting a story, it's important to consider what, if any, audience participation is expected during the telling. If the audience will be saying a repeated phrase, such as "Not I!" in "The Little Red Hen," let the audience know the signal that it's their turn to speak. This may be indicated by a pause and a nod by the storyteller or a hand gesture. The teller may want the audience to chant a repeated refrain, such as the song in "The Gunniwolf," included in this book.

RESPONDING TO THE AUDIENCE

The storyteller needs to be aware of the audience. Are the children getting restless? Do they seem to understand the story? If the teller sees puzzled looks, a specific word may need to be explained. Rather than making it a dictionary lesson, just tell the children what the word means. Is the area too hot or too cold? How's the noise level adjacent to the storytime area?

MISTAKES BEGINNERS MAKE

Bill Mooney and David Holt, on pages 77–83 of *The Storyteller's Guide*, list mistakes most commonly made by beginning storytellers:

- Selecting inappropriate stories for the age level
- Telling stories that are too long
- Telling the story too fast
- Using funny faces that detract from the story
- Getting ahead of the audience
- Thinking the story is funnier than it is
- Wandering around the room for no reason
- Apologizing for the story or telling
- Memorizing a story
- Being in love with the sound of your own voice

AUDIENCE RESPONSES

After telling the story, give the listeners a chance to let the story sink in. This is not the time to ask simple recall questions. The listeners want to experience a deeper understanding, not feel like they're being tested. One suggestion is to introduce the elements of folkore:

- Classic beginnings and endings (once upon a time, long ago, happily ever after)
- Magic
- Special people (kings, queens, elves, wise people, witches, giants, elves)

- Special numbers (3, 7, 12)
- Repetition of a phrase or song
- Anthropomorphism (animals that look and act like people)
- Good is rewarded and evil is punished
- Tasks to be performed

After you tell a story, ask the students to identify the elements of folklore that they noticed in the story.

For more ideas of ways to incorporate higher level thinking skills with folktales, see Chapter 8 of my book *Transforming Storytimes into Reading and Writing Lessons*.

It's time to turn to the stories in this book, choose one, prepare it, and tell it today!

Bibliography

Colum, Padraic. *Story Telling, Old and New*. 1927. New York: Macmillan, 1968.

Livo, Norma J., and Sandra A. Reitz. *Storytelling: Process and Practice*. Englewood Cliffs, NJ: Libraries Unlimited, 1986.

Mooney, Bill, and David Holt. *The Storyteller's Guide*. Little Rock, AR: August, 1996.

Weissman, Annie. *Transforming Storytimes into Reading and Writing Lessons*. Worthington, OH: Linworth, 2001.

Chapter 4 Using Proverbs to Tiptoe into Storytelling

Many people are scared away from storytelling because they are simply afraid to try it or they think an inordinate amount of time is necessary to learn a story. Starting with proverbs is a great way to dip into storytelling without much of a time investment or time "on stage."

Objectives for lessons based on proverbs come from the language arts and reading standards. Learning to read inferences and writing summaries of what is read are part of national and most state standards. The lesson plans below can be modified for Grades 2–8.

LESSON PLANS

Set

Recite a few proverbs that students will know such as "An apple a day keeps the doctor away." Ask students if they know them and what they mean.

Objectives

1. Students will infer meaning from proverbs.
2. Students will orally present material.

Whole Group Direct Instruction

State the meaning of the word "proverb" (a short popular saying that contains an important truth). Explain how proverbs originated (in the oral tradition, handed down through the generations) and why they evolved (to relate wisdom to future generations). Recite one of the proverbs from the list in this chapter. After you recite it, tell what you think it means. Example: "You can't unscramble eggs" (American proverb). It means that once you pierce the yolks and mix the yolks and whites of an egg together, you can't separate the yolks and whites. In other words, sometimes when something is done, it can't be undone.

Recite another proverb and ask students what the proverb means. Give students think time, and then ask them to tell their partner what they think it means. Call the group back to attention and ask a few students for their answers. Repeat several times until students understand what is required.

Guided Practice

Give each pair of students a proverb. Have the pair discuss the meaning of the proverb and take notes so they can make a presentation to the class. One student reads the proverb, and the other says its meaning. Have each pair present to the whole group.

Closure

Ask the students to tell their partner what a proverb is.

LESSON PLANS

Review

Ask a student to say a proverb from the day before. Have a volunteer state what it means.

Objective

Students will write the meaning of a specific proverb and how it relates to modern life.

Whole Group Direct Instruction

Recite a proverb from the list in this chapter. After you have recited it, tell what you think it means. Relate the meaning to modern life. Example: "If you cannot dance, you will say the drumming is poor" (African Proverb). This means that if you can't do something, it's easy to blame your failure on someone or something else. In modern life, this means if I don't do well in a class, I might say that the class was not interesting or the teacher was too hard.

Recite another proverb. Ask students what the proverb means and to relate it to modern life. Give students think time, and then ask them to discuss the two-part question with their partner. Call the group back to attention and ask a few students for their answers.

Using an overhead projector, smart board, or flip chart, write the first proverb you recited and its country of origin. Have the students assist in composing sentences for a paragraph on what the proverb means and how it relates to modern life.

Hand out a worksheet with the second proverb used. Give the students time to write a paragraph about what the proverb means and how it relates to modern life. Walk around monitoring to assess if students can do it.

Independent Practice

Give each student a proverb. Have students each write a paragraph about its meaning and how the proverb relates to modern life.

Closure

Have a few students share their proverbs and explanatory paragraphs.

ORAL PRESENTATION OF PROVERBS LESSON

LESSON PLANS

Set

State that making an oral presentation is on the list of top ten fears of Americans.

Objective

Students will orally present a proverb, its meaning, and its application to a small group of students.

Whole Group Direct Instruction

Use the information in Chapter 3 to tell and show students how to effectively give an oral presentation. Model one for students.

Guided Practice

Have each pair of students practice formally presenting their proverbs, meanings, and applications. Monitor their progress by walking around and listening to the practice.

Independent Practice

Combine pairs into groups of six and have each student present to the small group.

Closure

Have a few volunteers present their proverbs, meanings, and applications to the whole group.

SELECTED PROVERBS

The following are a few of the many proverbs that can be used in conjunction with geography and multicultural lessons and activities. Some of the books in the bibliography are from the adult section of the library. The easiest way to find books of proverbs is to search the 398.9 section of the school or public library.

From *Proverbs of Many Nations* compiled by Emery Kelen (New York: Lothrop, 1966)

"No matter how far you have gone on the wrong road, turn back." (Turkish)
"Be sure to keep an eye out for what you can swallow—and also for what can swallow you." (Telugu: India)
"Whoever lies down with a dog will get up with fleas." (Hebrew)
"The hungry will not fall asleep because someone else had enough to eat." (Swahili: Zanzibar)
"You can't unscramble eggs." (United States)
"It's one thing to cackle and another to lay an egg." (Ecuador)

From *Folk Wisdom of Mexico: Proverbios y Dichos Mexicanos* compiled by Jeff M. Sellers (San Francisco: Chronicle, 1994)

"The ill-mannered child finds a father everywhere he goes."
"El muchacho malcriado donde quiera encuentra padre."

"An ounce of gladness is worth more than an ounce of gold."
"Una onza del alegria vale mas que una onza de oro."

From *In Few Words/En pocas palabras* **by Jose Antonio Burciaga (San Francisco: Mercury, 1997)**
"A good life brings out wrinkles."
"Buena vida, arugas trae."

From *The Night Has Ears: African Proverbs* **by Ashley Bryan (New York: Atheneum, 1999)**
"If you cannot dance, you will say that the drumming is poor." (Ashanti)

From *Tigers, Frogs, and Rice Cakes: A Book of Korean Proverbs* **translated and selected by Daniel D. Holt (Auburn, CA: Shen's, 1999)**
"When whales fight, shrimps' backs are often broken."

From *The Facts on File Dictionary of Proverbs* **compiled by Rosalind Fergusson (New York: Facts on File, 1983)**
"The best mirror is an old friend."

Bibliography of Books of Proverbs

Berman, Louis A. *Proverb Wit & Wisdom.* New York: Berkeley, 1997.

Bryan, Ashley. *The Night Has Ears: African Proverbs.* New York: Atheneum, 1999.

Buchanan, Daniel Crump. *Japanese Proverbs and Sayings.* Norman, OK: U of Oklahoma, 1965.

Burciaga, Jose Antonio. *In Few Words/En pocas palabras.* San Francisco: Mercury, 1997.

Cobos, Ruben Refranes. *Southwestern Spanish Proverbs.* Santa Fe: Museum of New Mexico, 1985.

Fergusson, Rosalind, comp. *The Facts on File Dictionary of Proverbs.* New York: Facts On File, 1983.

Holt, Daniel D., trans. and selector. *Tigers, Frogs, and Rice Cakes: A Book of Korean Proverbs.* Auburn, CA: Shen's, 1999.

Kelen, Emery, comp. *Proverbs of Many Nations.* New York: Lothrop, 1966.

Kin, Kavid, ed. *Dictionary of American Maxims.* New York: Philosophical Library, 1960.

McDonald, Jule, comp. *Scottish Proverbs.* Iowa City, IA: Penfield, 1987.

Scheffler, Axel. *Let Sleeping Dogs Lie and Other Proverbs from Around the World.* Hauppauge, NY: Barron's, 1997.

Sellers, Jeff M., comp. *Folk Wisdom of Mexico: Proverbios y Dichos Mexicanos.* San Francisco: Chronicle, 1994.

Titelman, Gregory Y. *Random House Dictionary of Popular Proverbs & Sayings.* New York: Random House, 1996.

"Too Many Cooks..." and Other Proverbs. New York: Green Tiger, 1992.

Williams, Fionnuala. *Irish Proverbs.* Dublin: Poolberg, 1992.

Zona, Guy A. *The Soul Would Have No Rainbow If the Eyes Had No Tears and Other Native American Proverbs.* New York: Simon, 1994.

Chapter 5 Integrating Storytelling into the Library Storytime and School Curriculum without Going Crazy

Storytime in most libraries lasts twenty to thirty minutes. For the beginning storyteller, it is daunting to think of filling that time by telling stories. I recommend that an objective, based on national, state, or local curriculum standards, be the basis for the storytime. One story is told, and one or two books are read. In addition, an activity might be planned that supports the objective. This is a good and simple collaborative activity to use with teachers. You only need to know what curriculum standard is being studied at the time. Be sure to talk to the teacher about how you will be using storytelling to reinforce and extend classroom learning. This chapter has sample lessons that correlate with the stories that are in this book.

SOCIAL STUDIES AND LANGUAGE ARTS

The lessons on fables and myths can be used in conjunction with the study of Ancient Greece and Rome or reading comprehension lessons about main idea and theme. A Web site that has many of Aesop's and La Fontaine's fables is <http://www.AesopFables.com>. The tall tale lessons can be used in conjunction with American history units or language arts narrative writing lessons. Paul Bunyan stories are on the Web at <http://www.newnorth.net/~bmorren/bunyan.html>. Stories about Annie Christmas, Pecos Bill, Paul Bunyan, Casey Jones, and Mike Fink can be found at <http://www.thinkquest.org/library/lib/site_sum_outside.html?tname=J001779&turl=J001779/stories1.htm>.

FABLES

LESSON PLANS *Day 1: Introducing Fables*

Review and Set

Ask students what advice they remember getting from parents or teachers.

Objectives

1. Students will demonstrate understanding that a fable is a teaching story that uses anthropomorphic animals as characters.
2. Students will infer the moral or teaching message from a folktale and relate it to life today.

Whole Group Direct Instruction

Explain that fables are stories that were told to teach adults and children lessons. One of the most famous authors of fables is Aesop. He lived in ancient Greece. He was born a slave, about 620 B.C. He was given his freedom as a reward for his learning. Most of the characters in his fables are anthropomorphic animals, ones that act like people. Tell the students that you are going to tell and read fables. They are to figure out what the "lesson" or "moral" is.

Tell one of Aesop's Fables, such as the "The Rooster and the Jewel."

Model how to say the fable's lesson and how to explain why that is the lesson: "The moral of the story is that the things which are very valuable to one person have no value for another person. The rooster couldn't use a jewel. He couldn't get food for it. A grain of corn was worth much more to him because it would keep him alive. These days, there are many yard sales. People clean out their things and decide what they don't want anymore. Buyers, who come to the yard sales, find 'treasures' among the things the sellers want to get rid of at a low price, because they aren't valuable to the sellers."

Guided Practice

Remind the students that they should be listening to figure out the lesson of the fable. Read another fable from one of the books in the bibliography after the fable lessons. Ask students what the lesson of the fable is, why it is the lesson, and how the lesson relates to life today. Give them think time. After think time, pair them up and have the students tell their partners their answers in a soft voice. Circulate and listen in on the sharing. Call the group to attention. Have some of the pairs share their lessons of the story and tell why they are the lessons. Repeat with another fable if time permits.

Closure

Have students chorally answer these questions: Why did people tell fables? (to teach a lesson) Who are usually the characters in a fable? (animals) Do the animals act like people or animals? (people)

Day 2: Fables

Review

Ask students, "What are the elements of fables?" (animals act as people; they are meant to teach a lesson)

Objective

Students will infer the moral or teaching message from a fable and relate it to life today.

Whole Group Direct Instruction

Tell the students that you are going to tell and read fables, one by Aesop, one by La Fontaine (a Frenchman who wrote in the 1600s), and a modern fable by Arnold Lobel. Students are to figure out what the "lesson" or "moral" is.

Tell "The North Wind and the Sun" and then read a fable from one of the books in the bibliography. Remind the students that they are to figure out the lesson of the story. Do the guided practice after each fable is presented.

Guided Practice

After each fable, ask students what the lesson of the fable is, why it is the lesson, and how it relates to life today. Give them think time. After think time, pair them up and have the students tell their partners their answers, in a quiet six-inch voice. Circulate and listen in on the sharing. Call the group to attention. Have some of the pairs share their lessons of the story and tell why they are the lessons. Repeat with the other fables.

Closure

Have students chorally answer these questions: Why did people tell fables? (to teach a lesson) Who are usually the characters in a fable? (animals) Do the animals act like people or animals? (people)

Day 3: Composing Fables

Review

Ask students, "What are the elements of fables?" (animals act as people; they are meant to teach a lesson)

Objective

Students will use interactive writing with the instructor to compose a fable to illustrate a lesson provided to them.

Whole Group Direct Instruction

Tell the students a fable and the lesson that goes with it. Then tell the class that you will compose a fable to fit a lesson, then they will write one with you. Using a white or smart board, chart, or overhead projector, write the lesson "Don't talk to strangers." Model how to write a fable to illustrate the lesson. Pick two animals, with one being the predator of the other, such as a mouse and a snake. Write a fable such as:

> Once there lived a mother mouse who had two children. The mother mouse warned her children about dangers in the world outside their nest. The young mice went to look for some cheese, but came scurrying back home.
>
> "Mother, there is a big thing with wings that swooped down near us. We ran away. Is that a stranger?"
>
> "Yes, children. That stranger is an owl. Owls like to eat mice, so stay away from owls."
>
> The young mice went out later to look for food. The younger one boasted, "I'm not afraid of strangers. I want to meet everyone."
>
> A snake slithered over to the two mice. The older mouse remembered the owl. "Let's run home!" he cried.
>
> "You run along if you're scared," said the younger mouse. "I'm going to talk to the snake."
>
> As the older mouse ran home, he looked back just as the snake swallowed his brother.
>
> The lesson is "Don't talk to strangers."

Guided Practice

State a lesson for a class fable, such as "Be wary of those who flatter you." Ask the students for ideas for animals for the fable. Choose the two that seem the most likely to match the lesson. Ask the students what situation will give meaning to this lesson. Give them think time. After think time, pair them up and have the students tell their partners their answers. Circulate and listen in on the sharing. Call the group to attention. Have some of the pairs share their ideas. Choose one of the ideas and have the students compose the lead sentence using the "pair share" strategy. Write the lead sentence on the white or smart board, overhead projector, or chart. Use the same method to write a one-paragraph fable.

Closure

Have students chorally read the fable they have just composed. Point out the salient characteristics: animal characters act like people and a plot leads to the "lesson."

Day 4: Writing Fables

Review

What are the elements of fables? (animals act as people; they are meant to teach a lesson)

Objective

Students will write a fable to go with a lesson.

Whole Group Direct Instruction

Tell the students a fable and have them figure out, using "pair share," the lesson that goes with it and how it relates to life today.

Remind the students of the "lesson" for which they wrote the fable on the previous day. Have the students chorally read the fable. Remind them of the steps in writing the fable:

1. Decide on two animal characters.
2. Brainstorm situations to show the need for the "lesson."
3. Compose the lead sentence and then other sentences.
4. Make sure the fable will bring the reader to the "lesson."

Guided Practice

Give the students a lesson, such as "Don't put off until tomorrow what you can do today," about which to write a fable. Have the students brainstorm with a partner about the animals and situations.

Independent Practice

Have the students write the fable. Remind them to make it short and to the point.

Closure

Have a few of the students read their fables. After each, point out the elements: anthropomorphic animals and the "lesson."

Bibliography of Books of Fables

Aesop's Fables illustrated by Charles Santore. New York: Jelly Bean, 1988.

Aesop's Fables based on the translation of George Flyer Townsend. New York: Doubleday, 1968.

Aesop's Fables illustrated by Lisbeth Zwerger. Saxonville, MA: Picture Book Studio, 1989.

Anno, Mitsumasa. *Anno's Aesop.* New York: Orchard, 1987.

Calmenson, Stephanie. *The Children's Aesop.* Honesdale, PA: Caroline, 1992.

Clark, Margaret. *The Best of Aesop's Fables.* Boston: Little, 1990.

Fables of Aesop adapted and illustrated by Tom Lynch. New York: Viking, 2000.

Hague, Michael. *Aesop's Fables.* New York: Holt, 1985.

Lobel, Arnold. *Fables.* New York: Harper, 1980.

McClintock, Barbara. *Animal Fables from Aesop.* Boston: Godine, 1991.

Orgel, Doris. *The Lion and the Mouse and Other Aesop's Fables.* New York: DK, 2000.

Pinkney, Jerry. *Aesop's Fables.* New York: Seastar, 2000.

Stevens, Janet. *The Town Mouse and the Country Mouse: An Aesop's Fable.* New York: Holiday, 1987.

MYTHS

These lessons can be used with the study of Ancient Greece and Rome or with language arts classes studying myths. The Greek myth lesson can also be used with classes studying Shakespeare's *Romeo and Juliet*. Myths are especially appropriate for sixth grade and up.

LESSON PLANS

Lesson 1: The Greek Myth "Pyramus and Thisbe"

Review and Set

Ask students, "How many of you have seen the Romeo and Juliet movies? One starred Leonardo DiCaprio and was set in a modern city. Another modern day version of *Romeo and Juliet* was the movie and musical *West Side Story.*"

Objectives

1. Students will be able to discuss how coincidences can determine the action in a plot.
2. Students will relate the story of Pyramus and Thisbe to life today.

Whole Group Direct Instruction

Tell students that sometimes a coincidence has a huge consequence in a story. As you tell the story "Pyramus and Thisbe," you want students to think about what the coincidences were and the consequences of those coincidences. Tell the story. After telling the story, point out one coincidence (there was a crack in the wall) and how it affected the story (the lovers could communicate and agree to meet).

Guided Practice

Ask students to determine at least three other coincidences in the myth and how they influenced the outcome of the story. Give them think time. After think time, pair them up and have the students compare their answers, in a six-inch voice. Circulate and listen in on the sharing. Call the group to attention. Have some of the pairs share their ideas. Repeat the same strategy with the next question: Could this kind of love story happen today? Why or why not?

Closure

Summarize students' comments that show how old myths can reveal things that are true today.

Lesson 2: Roman Myths

Review and Set

Ask students, "How many of you have seen television programs in which 'makeovers' are given to people?" Briefly describe how the makeover was done.

Objective

Students will relate the story "Pygmalion" to the idea of nature versus nurture, using critical thinking skills.

Whole Group Direct Instruction

Tell the story "Pygmalion." After telling the story, briefly explain the premise of George Bernard Shaw's play *Pygmalion*. (A professor of languages teaches a girl with bad grammar and pronunciation to speak correctly so that she is taken for a princess at a social gathering. He falls in love with her.)

Guided Practice

Ask the students why George Bernard Shaw called the play *Pygmalion*. Ask how the play related to the myth. Give students think time. After think time, pair up students, and have the students compare their answers. Circulate and listen in on the sharing. Call the group to attention. Have some of the pairs share the lessons of the story and tell why they are the lessons of the story. Repeat the same "pair share" strategy with the next questions: Are people changed by what they are taught and how they are treated? If someone creates a "Pygmalion," what does that mean?

Closure

Say to students, "Today I told you a Roman myth that has influenced modern literature. What is the name of the myth?" (Choral response of *"Pygmalion."*)

Bibliography of Books of Greek and Roman Myths

Bulfinch, Thomas. *Bulfinch's Mythology*. New York: Harper, 1991.

Hutton, Warwick. *Theseus and the Minotaur*. New York: McElderry, 1989.

Lasky, Kathryn. *Hercules*. New York: Hyperion, 1997.

McCaughrean, Geraldine. *Roman Myths*. New York: McElderry, 2001.

Mayer, Mariana. *Pegasus*. New York: Morrow, 1998.

Morley, Jacqaueline. *Greek Myths*. New York: Peter Bedrick, 1997.

Osborne, Mary Pope. *Favorite Greek Myths*. New York: Scholastic, 1989.

Osborne, Mary Pope. *Favorite Norse Myths*. New York: Scholastic, 1996.

Tomaino, Sarah F. *Persephone Bringer of Spring*. New York: Crowell, 1971.

TALL TALES

| LESSON PLANS | *Lesson 1* |

Review and Set

Say to students, "Sometimes I exaggerate to make a point. Most people do. For instance, I might say I had to stay up all night to finish my homework or that I danced all night or that I had to walk five miles to school. What exaggerations have you said lately?"

Objective

Students will be able to analyze a tall tale for exaggeration and heroic qualities.

Whole Group Direct Instruction

Say to students, "There are stories in American literature called *tall tales*. These are exaggerated stories about imaginary heroes and heroines. Sometimes the stories explain natural or man-made phenomena. The story is usually about a person who does extraordinary things in the service of others. I'm going to tell you a tall tale and then read you one. I want you to be thinking about what is exaggerated in the story and what the main character is like by his appearance, by what he said, and by what he did." Tell "Pecos Bill."

Guided Practice

Ask the students, "What were three of the exaggerations in the story—the things that were made much more than they could have really been?" Give them think time. After think time, pair them up and have them compare their answers with their partners in a soft voice. Circulate and listen in on the sharing. Call the group to attention. Have some of the pairs share their exaggerations in the story and tell why they are exaggerations.

Ask the students to describe Pecos Bill by what he looked like, said, and did. Use the same "pair share" strategy. Ask the students what are some of the qualities and actions that made Pecos Bill a hero. Use "pair share" to discuss.

Read *Mike Fink* by Steven Kellogg. Ask the same questions and use the same strategies.

Closure

Ask students, "What is one thing that a tall tale has?" (Expect the choral answer *exaggeration*.)

Lesson 2: Tall Tales

Review

Say to students, "Last time, I told and read you the tall tales "Pecos Bill" and *Mike Fink*. What are some of the elements in a tall tale?" (exaggeration, hero)

Objective

Students will brainstorm and compose together a modern tall tale.

Whole Group Direct Instruction

Tell the tall tale "Paul Bunyan." Have the students identify the exaggerations and character traits of the hero with the same questions and strategies of Lesson 1.

Guided Practice

Tell the students that together you will brainstorm ideas for a modern tall tale. Tell them to think of a current problem that needs to be fixed. Make a few suggestions, such as polluted air and crowded highways. Give them think time. Then have them tell their partners the ideas. Call the students back to attention and ask for their ideas. Write them on a smart or white board, over-

head projector, or large chart. Allow some discussion, and then pick the one that seems the most viable.

Tell the students that now they need to think up a "larger-than-life" character to solve the problem. Give them think time. Have the pairs share their ideas with the rest of the class, and choose the one that best fits the problem.

Say, "Let's get to know this character. What exaggerations can we make about the character's appearance, speech, and deeds?" Use "pair share" to solicit ideas. Write them all down, and then circle the ones that fit best.

Say, "How is this character, this hero, going to solve the problem we set?" Use "pair share" to solicit ideas.

Closure

Say, "Today, we brainstormed a modern tall tale that had exaggeration by creating a heroic character who solved a superhuman problem. What were some of the exaggerations? What was the problem and what was the solution?"

Bibliography of Books of American Tall Tales

Brooke, William J. *A Telling of the Folktales: Five Stories.* New York: Harper, 1990.

Emberley, Barbara. *The Story of Paul Bunyan.* Englewood Cliffs, NJ: Prentice-Hall, 1963.

Gleeson, Brian. *Pecos Bill.* Saxonville, MA: Rabbit Ears, 1988.

Kellogg, Steven. *Pecos Bill: A Tall Tale.* New York: Morrow, 1986.

Kellogg, Steven. *Mike Fink: A Tall Tale.* New York: Morrow, 1992.

Osborne, Mary Pope. *American Tall Tales.* New York: Knopf, 1991.

Rounds, Glen. *Ol' Paul, The Mighty Logger.* New York: Holiday, 1976.

San Souci, Robert D. *Larger Than Life: The Adventures of American Legendary Heroes.* New York: Doubleday, 1991.

Stoutenburg, Adrien. *American Tall Tales.* New York: Penguin, 1976.

Walker, Paul Robert. *Big Men, Big Country.* San Diego: Harcourt, 1993.

Wright, Catherine. *Steamboat Annie and the Thousand Pound Catfish.* New York: Philomel, 2001.

MATHEMATICS

Cognitively Guided Instruction

One philosophy for teaching mathematics to kindergarteners through third graders is Cognitively Guided Instruction (CGI), developed at the University of Wisconsin at Madison and funded by the National Science Foundation. CGI fits particularly well with storytelling, as it is a word problem–based program.

Children's Mathematics: Cognitively Guided Instruction by Thomas P. Carpenter et al. specifies types of problems and students' strategies for solving them. In order to combine this with storytelling, some supplies are necessary. At least 24 counters of any type, such as poker chips, unifix cubes, beans, and so on, should be provided to pairs of students. For the library, these are best kept in either plastic zipper bags or small pencil boxes. The latter has the advantage of affording a surface on which the students can work.

One of the overriding principles of CGI is that students develop strategies for solving problems and that these should be shared with others. For all of the following lessons, it is important to give students the counters, to listen in on their conversations with their partners, and to have some of them share not only the answer but how the problem was solved. Note there is no modeling or "guided practice" in these lessons because the students are to figure out their own strategies and construct new knowledge based on these. These lessons are appropriate for grades kindergarten through third grade.

Each lesson also has a picture book read-aloud with CGI math problems. These were designed by Susan Garvin, a collaborative peer teacher and teacher-librarian in the Roosevelt School District, in Phoenix, Arizona. She has graciously allowed me to incorporate her work into the following lesson plans.

MATHEMATICS

LESSON PLANS

Review
Say to students, "In your math classes, you've done word problems—math questions that are told primarily with words, not numbers. You have to figure out how to solve the problem."

Objective
Students will be able to solve word problems based on stories told or read, without using paper and pencil.

Lesson Plan 1

Whole Group Direct Instruction
Tell the story "The Three Billy Goats Gruff."

Students' Strategies Practice
Give out the counters to each pair of students. Pose this problem: "If there were three Billy Goats Gruff, and the first one got across the bridge safely, how many were left on the other side?" The students work on the problem together, telling their partners how to solve it. Monitor the pairs. Call the students back to attention. Repeat the problem and ask for a choral answer. Call on several students to explain how they got the answer.

Using the same method, pose the following problems based on "The Three Billy Goats Gruff."

- If there were three Billy Goats Gruff and two got across the bridge safely, how many were left?
- The biggest Billy Goat Gruff ate six clumps of grass. The middle Billy Goat Gruff ate four clumps of grass. How many clumps of grass did they eat together?
- The biggest Billy Goat Gruff ate six clumps of grass. The smallest Billy Goat Gruff ate two clumps of grass. How many more clumps of grass did the biggest Billy Goat Gruff eat?
- The three Billy Goats Gruff met their four cousins on the hillside. How many billy goats were there in all?

Have the students put the counters back in the containers. Read *Three Cheers for Tacky* by Helen Lester (Boston: Houghton Mifflin, 1994). Have the students take out the counters again and work in pairs to solve some of the following problems. (You fill in the blanks with numbers before posing the problems.)

- There were ___ penguins on an iceberg. They each had two flippers. How many flippers were there altogether?
- Tacky caught ___ fish for lunch and dinner. He ate ___ fish for lunch. How many fish did he have left for dinner?
- The penguins practiced their cheers ___ times on Monday and ___ times on Tuesday. How many times did they practice altogether?
- There were ___ cheering teams at the contest. There were ___ penguins in each team. How many penguins were there altogether at the contest?
- There were ___ flowers on Tacky's Hawaiian shirt. Each flower had ___ petals. How many flower petals were on Tacky's shirt?

■ Lovely had ____ polka dots on his bow tie and Neatly had ____ more than Lovely. How many polka dots did Neatly have on his bow tie?

Closure

Say to students, "Today we solved math problems based on "The Three Billy Goat Gruff" and *Three Cheers for Tacky*. Can you think of a problem based on one of these stories?" Solicit a few answers.

Lesson Plan 2

Review

Say, "In your math classes, you've done word problems—math questions that are told primarily with words, not numbers. You have to figure out how to solve the problem."

Objective

Students will be able to solve word problems based on stories, without using paper and pencil.

Whole Group Direct Instruction

Tell the story "The Wide-Mouthed Frog."

Students' Strategies Practice

Put the students in pairs and pass out the counters. Tell the students that you are going to pose word problems about "The Wide-Mouthed Frog," and they are to discuss with their partner how to solve the problem and come up with the answer. Monitor the pairs. Call the students back to attention. Repeat the problem and ask for a choral answer. Call on several students to explain how they got the answer. Problems:

■ The wide-mouthed frog talked to five animals. Each of them gave him two suggestions on what to feed his babies. How many suggestions did he get?
■ The wide-mouthed frog's wife had six babies. Her sister had four babies. How many more babies did the wide-mouthed frog's wife have than her sister?
■ The snake stole four eggs from one nest and seven eggs from another nest. How many eggs did he have for his babies?
■ The owl's six babies ate mice. They spit out twelve bones. How many bones did each spit out?

Have the students put the counters back in the containers before reading *My Little Sister Ate One Hare* by Bill Grossman (New York: Scholastic, 1996). Pose some of the following problems, filling in the blanks with numbers. Students should discuss their strategies with their partners and may use the counters if they wish.

■ The little sister ate ____ ants, ____ shrews, and ____ bats. How many animals did she eat altogether?
■ The little sister ate ____ worms but spit up ____ of them. How many worms were left in her stomach?
■ The little sister ate ____ lizards. ____ were brown and the rest were green. How many green lizards did she eat?
■ The little sister had ____ jars to catch polliwogs. If each jar could hold ____ polliwogs, how many polliwogs could she catch and put in the jars?
■ The little sister ate ____ bats. She also ate ____ pieces of clothing of each bat. How many pieces of bat clothing did she eat altogether?

Chapter 5: Integrating Storytelling into the Library Storytime and School Curriculum without Going Crazy   29

■ The little sister had some mice. She went to the woods and caught ____ more mice. Now she has ____ mice. How many mice did she have to start with?

■ The little sister ate ____ worms. How many more worms does she need to eat to have eaten ____ worms?

Closure

Have the students make up a problem from one of the stories.

Bibliography for Math Lessons

Carpenter, Thomas P. *Children's Mathematics: Cognitively Guided Instruction*. Portsmouth, NH: Heinemann, 1999.

Grossman, Bill. *My Little Sister Ate One Hare*. New York: Scholastic, 1996.

Lester, Helen. *Three Cheers for Tacky*. Boston: Houghton Mills, 1994.

LANGUAGE ARTS AND READING COMPREHENSION

LESSON PLANS

Lesson 1

Review and Set

Ask, "What did you do before you came to school today?" After a few actions are stated, like "ate breakfast," "got dressed," "woke up," and "took a shower," restate them in nonsensical order such as "I got dressed, I took a shower, and then I got up." Explain that events have to be in some order, in life or in a story, to make sense.

Objective

Students will act out the story "Henny Penny" with the correct sequence of events.

Whole Group Direct Instruction

Tell the story "Henny Penny." Tell the students that they are going to act it out. Choose students to play Cocky Locky, Ducky Lucky, Goosey Lucy, Turkey Lurky, and Foxy Loxy. Play Henny Penny yourself. Retell the story, prompting the actors in their parts. An alternative is to have the "audience" say the part with the character. Everyone should say the refrains "Where are you going Henny Penny?" and "We are going to the king, to tell him that the sky is falling!"

Act out the story several times with different actors.

Guided Instruction

Divide the class into groups of four students. Give each group a set of the characters. (These can be copied from the set in Chapter 6, Board Storytelling.) The groups are to put the characters in the order in which they come in the story.

Closure

Ask the groups to chorally answer who came first, next, and so on. *Note:* The same lesson can be repeated with other stories, such a "The Little Red Hen" and "The Three Wishes."

Lesson 2

Review and Set

Say, "Whenever we come into a new situation, we compare it to what we know. We think about how it is the same as, and how it is different from, what we know. For instance, when you go to a new place, you think about these things: Is this place as hot or cold, or as rainy or sunny, as where I live? Does this place have as many people as where I live? Are the plants the same or different? Today, we're going to compare stories and say what's the same and what's different about them."

Objective

Students will compare two stories.

Whole Group Direct Instruction

Tell students that while you are telling and reading stories to them, they are to listen for things that are the same and things that are different between (or among) the stories. Tell the story listed below and read the book that is paired with it.

Guided Practice

Ask the students to think of three things that are the same in the two stories. If you ask for one response, it will most likely be a surface one. Thinking of three responses will require the students to think more deeply. After think time, partner the students and have them share with their partner the three things that are the same. Monitor the pairs. Call the students back to attention and have them share their answers. If a writing component is desired, make a Venn diagram, as shown in the sample below, and write the things that are the same in the middle. Repeat the strategy for three things that are different. Write these in the separate circles.

Model the writing activity. For the pairing of "The Teeny Tiny Woman" and *The Little Old Lady Who Wasn't Afraid of Anything*, the topic sentence is: *"The Teeny Tiny Woman" and* The Little Old Lady Who Wasn't Afraid of Anything *are similar in some ways.* The supporting sentences are: *Both are scary stories that have a woman as the main character. In both stories the women go for a walk. Both stories have magic and repetition in them. Both women are not scared at the end.* The topic sentence of the next paragraph is: *There are differences between the stories.* The next sentence is: *In "The Teeny Tiny Woman," the woman brings the bone home herself, she lives in town, and the audience is scared at the end.* The second sentence is: *In* The Little Old Lady Who Wasn't Afraid of Anything, *the major differences are that the pieces of a man appear and that she lives in the forest.*

Closure

If it was a listening comprehension activity, summarize the things that the students found the same and different about the stories. If the lesson had the writing component, have the students chorally read the paragraphs composed.

Venn Diagram

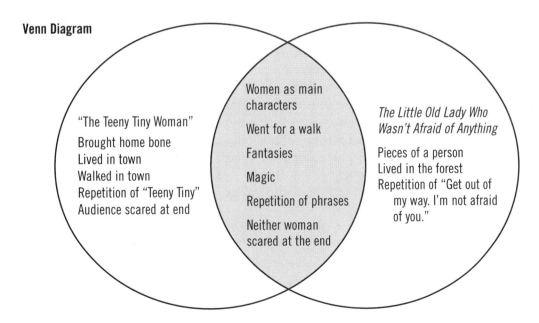

"The Teeny Tiny Woman"
Brought home bone
Lived in town
Walked in town
Repetition of "Teeny Tiny"
Audience scared at end

Women as main characters

Went for a walk

Fantasies

Magic

Repetition of phrases

Neither woman scared at the end

The Little Old Lady Who Wasn't Afraid of Anything

Pieces of a person
Lived in the forest
Repetition of "Get out of my way. I'm not afraid of you."

Story Told	Book(s) Read
The Little Red Hen	Stevens, Janet. *Cook-A-Doodle-Do.* San Diego: Harcourt, 1999. Sturges, Philemon. *Little Red Hen Makes a Pizza.* Dutton, 1999.
Henny Penny	Hest, Amy. *In the Rain with Baby Duck.* Cambridge, MA: Candlewick, 1998. Kasza, Keiko. *Wolf's Chicken Stew.* New York: Putnam, 1987. Root, Phyllis. *One Duck Stuck.* Cambridge, MA: Candlewick, 1998.
The Teeny Tiny Woman	Williams, Linda. *The Little Old Lady Who Wasn't Afraid of Anything.* New York: Crowell, 1986. Loredo, Elizabeth. *Boogie Bones.* New York: Putnam, 1997.
The Three Wishes	Kimmel, Eric A. *Anansi and the Moss Covered Rock.* New York: Holiday, 1988. Steig, William. *Sylvester and the Magic Pebble.* 1969. New York: Simon, 1980.
Escaped Maniac	Shannon, George. *Stories to Solve: Folktales From Around the World.* New York: Beech Tree, 1991.
Followed Home	Poe, Edgar Allan. *The Tell-Tale Heart and Other Writings.* New York: Bantam, 1982. Shannon, George. *More Stories to Solve: Fifteen Folktales from Around the World.* New York: Greenwillow, 1990.
The Gunniwolf	Hyman, Trina Shart. *Little Red Riding Hood.* New York: Holiday, 1983. Young, Ed. *Lon Po Po: A Red-Riding Hood Story from China.* New York: Philomel, 1989.
The Frog Prince	Galdone, Paul. *Rumpelstiltskin.* New York: Clarion, 1985. Zelinsky, Paul O. *Rapunzel.* New York: Dutton, 1998.
Paul Bunyan	Isaacs, Anne. *Swamp Angel.* New York: Dutton, 1994. Williams, Suzanne. *Library Lil.* New York: Dial, 1997.
The Golden Arm	Galdone, Joanna. *Tailypo.* New York: Seabury, 1977. Medearis, Angela Shelf. *Tailypo: A New Fangled Folk Tale.* New York: Holiday, 1996.
La Llorona	Anaya, Rudolfo. *Maya's Children: The Story of La Llorona.* New York: Hyperion, 1997.
The Three Billy Goats Gruff	Aardema, Verna. *Borreguita and the Coyote: A Tale from Ayutla, Mexico.* New York: Knopf, 1991. Grimm, Jacob. *The Wolf and the Seven Little Kids.* New York: North-South, 1995.
The Wide-Mouthed Frog	Kalen, Robert. *Jump, Frog, Jump.* New York: Greenwillow, 1995. London, Jonathan. *Froggy Gets Dressed.* New York: Viking, 1992.
Two Ranching Families	McLerran, Alice. *Year of the Ranch.* New York: Viking, 1996. Raczek, Linda Theres. *The Night the Grandfathers Danced.* Flagstaff, AZ: Northland, 1995.

LANGUAGE ARTS AND THE WRITING PROCESS

These lessons use storytelling to model narrative structure. It's unrealistic to think that the students would go through the entire writing process (prewriting, drafting, revising, editing, and publishing) to write individual stories in the library. Rather, this group of lessons is meant to be a collaborative effort between the teacher-librarian and the classroom teacher. The teacher-librarian can do the lessons below. The third lesson shows how to illustrate a class story to publish as a big book. Instead of a big book, another idea is to type the story and make a copy, with room for pictures, for each student. The students can illustrate these in the classroom, where they practice reading the story. When the books are completed, the students take them home and read them to their families.

LESSON PLANS

Lesson 1: Structure of a Narrative Story

Review

Say to students, "Narrative stories have a beginning, a middle, and an end. The last time you were here, we read (insert a book read previously). In the beginning of that book, (insert what happened at the beginning). In the middle of that book, (insert what happened in the middle). At the end of that book, (insert what happened at the end)."

Objectives

1. Students will be able to identify the beginning, middle, and end of stories told and read to them.
2. Students will brainstorm ideas for the beginning and middle of a modern version of "The Three Wishes."

Whole Group Direct Instruction

Say, "Today you're going to hear a story and then figure out what happened in the beginning, the middle, and the end." Tell "The Three Wishes." Ask the students what happened at the beginning, middle, and end. Have them respond by using the "pair share" strategy. (Beginning: The woodcutter is granted three wishes. Middle: He and his wife can't decide on a wish and waste their wishes by first asking for a sausage, then for the sausage to be on his nose. Ending: The woodcutter and his wife wished for the sausage to be back on the plate, and they had to make do with what they had.)

Guided Practice

Use brainstorming as a prewriting activity to write a modern version of the story. Ask each question below, and then use "pair share," a strategy explained after the first question, to get students' suggestions. Write the suggestions on a smart or white board, transparency on an overhead projector, or a large chart.

1. "We'll start with the beginning. Today, not many people are woodcutters. What kind of job might give a person a chance to save an elf or someone with magic power?" Give students think time. Assign partners and have the students discuss the question. Bring the students back to attention and have them share their ideas. Choose one of the jobs that makes the most sense.
2. "Now we'll go to the middle. Who besides a husband or wife could we put in the story to share the wishes?" Choose one.
3. "What kinds of wishes would these characters think of and argue about?" Choose three or four.
4. "What food should the main character wish for?" Choose one food.
5. "Where should the angry character wish for the food to go?"
6. "Now we're ready for the end. What will the two main characters agree the third wish will be?"

Closure

Have the students read, from the circled notes, the name and job of the main character, the other character, what they argued about wishing for, and what food the main character wished for.

Lesson 2: Narrative Writing Structure

Review

Say, "Narrative stories have a beginning, a middle, and an end. The last time you were here, I told you 'The Three Wishes.' The beginning was when the woodcutter is granted three wishes. The middle was when he and his wife couldn't decide on a wish and wasted their wishes by asking first for a sausage and then for the sausage to be on his nose. The end was when the woodcutter and his wife wished for the sausage to be back on the table and had to make do with what they had. We started a modern version of that story." Put up the notes from the last lesson. Ask, "What was the beginning?" (Students say what happened in the beginning.) "What was the middle?" (Students say what happened in the middle.) "What was the end?" (Students say what happened at the end.)

Objective

Students will compose the sentences for a modern version of "The Three Wishes."

Whole Group Direct Instruction

Use interactive writing to write the story:

"Today you're going to write the sentences for our modern story of 'The Three Wishes.' Let's start with the title page. What's the title?" (choral response of "The Three Wishes") "Who is writing the story?" (We are!) "Yes, I'll put written by the students in M——'s class."

"Let's start with the beginning. How do most folktales start?" (Once upon a time) "Yes, let's start that way. So our sentence will be, 'Once upon a time there was a ___'" (Students give the character chorally) "who was ___ ... What was he doing?" (Students supply from notes.)

1. "How did he or she get the wishes? That's the beginning of the story. Think about how we could say that in a sentence." (Use "pair share" to come up with ideas for the next sentences.)
2. "Now we need a new paragraph for the middle. What happens in the middle of our story?" (They argue over wish suggestions, they wish for food, and then one character wishes food on the other's nose.) Divide the group into three sets of pairs and have each set of pairs work on one of the three sets of sentences, one sentence for each event.
3. "Now we're ready for the end. The last sentence of the original story was, 'The woodcutter and his wife ate the sausage for dinner. And it was tasty!' What do we want the last sentence to be?" (Students use "pair share" to come up with ideas.)

Closure

Have the students read their story chorally.

Before this lesson, type the new version of "The Three Wishes" using a font size of at least 16 points. Print the story and cut the text into "chunks" for illustration. These text chunks, as well as paper and crayons, should be set on the library tables.

Lesson 3: Narrative Writing Structure

Review

Have the students chorally read the modern version of "The Three Wishes" that they wrote in the previous lesson.

Objective

Students will illustrate a particular passage of the story they wrote for the previous lesson.

Whole Group Direct Instruction

Say, "Today we're going to illustrate our story. This means each person will draw a picture to show what's going on in the words that are on your paper. Several people will be drawing for the same words. Make sure to write your name on your paper." Take one text chunk and read it. Say, "What could be drawn to show this?"

Guided Practice

Read the text chunks to the students who cannot read them. Then have the students illustrate the text. Remember to paperclip the text chunks to the illustrations!

Closure

Have the students chorally read the story again. *Note:* Make the big book by pasting the text chunks on 9- × 12-inch construction paper. Cut out the students' illustrations with their names, and affix them to the correct text chunk. Extra illustrations can be used for the cover and title page. The book lasts longer if the front and back cover are laminated before it is bound.

Chapter 6 Board Storytelling

HOW BOARD STORYTELLING DIFFERS FROM TRADITIONAL STORYTELLING

Board storytelling can be done on a felt board, flannelboard, or magnetic board or with a fabric and Velcro apron. The techniques for telling are the same for all of these. The only difference is how the characters are made.

Board storytelling differs from traditional storytelling in that there are visual aids for the audience and the teller. This can be very helpful when telling stories to English language learners. By pointing to the board figures as the story is told, the students can link the verbal input with the picture. Board storytelling is also easier for the teller to remember, as there are figures to jog the memory for the next event. It's helpful to number the back of the figures so they are easy to check for order. It is distressing to start telling a board story and then to have to fumble around for the correct character because the pieces are out of order.

A special effort must be made to focus on the audience when telling board stories. Many people make the mistake of facing the board instead of the audience. Stand to the side of the board, not in front of it, when telling the story. As it's time to put up a figure for the story, turn to the board, put it up, and then turn back to face the audience. If you want the audience to say a repetitive part of the story with you, point to the figure and pause, but keep your eyes on the audience. Sometimes it's easier to do this by standing in back of the board. For instance, in "The Little Red Hen," point to the cat, the dog, and the pig to encourage the audience to say, "Not I!" For "Henny Penny," point to the animals as they go on their way, having the students name them as you point to the characters.

CRITERIA FOR GOOD BOARD STORIES

Stories told with a board should be short and simple, with a definite sequence of events. The figures should have clean lines so that they are comprehensible even to those students sitting the farthest from the board. The patterns for "The Little Red Hen" and "Henny Penny" are included in this chapter. These stories are included in Chapter 9 of this book.

TYPES OF BOARDS

Magnetic boards are available through many teaching-supply vendors. Many new classrooms have white boards affixed to the wall that are also magnetic. Magnetic strips and dots are available at hardware and craft stores. Some are self-adhesive. To make the figures, copy the patterns onto card stock. Color the patterns with crayon, paint, markers, or colored pencils. Make sure they are bright enough to be seen by children who are sitting the farthest back in the story area. Cut out the figures, cutting widely around feet or other narrow areas. Place the magnetic strip toward the top of the figures, with a small piece at the bottom to guard against roll up. If the magnet strips aren't self-adhesive, use a glue gun to secure in place.

Fabric boards can be bought or made from felt, flannel, or Polartec material. The covered board should be at least 18 × 24 inches to allow enough room to tell different stories. A box won't do because the flannel board must be situated at an angle to be effective. (A box would need to be cut so it is a single sheet.) The board is then propped up against books or a shelf, or it is set on an easel. Aprons can also be made of Polartec. The patterns for the figures can be copied onto regular paper or card stock, then colored with crayons, paint, markers, or colored pencils. Make sure they are bright enough to be seen by children who are sitting the farthest back in the story area. Cut out the figures, cutting widely around feet or other narrow areas. Paste strips of felt on the back of the figures, or stick on the self-adhesive felt tape, available from teaching-supply vendors, toward the top of the figures, with a small piece at the bottom to guard against roll-up. A Polartec board or apron requires that Velcro be used on the back of the figures.

Bibliography of Books for Beginner Board Stories

Anderson, Paul S. *Storytelling with the Flannel Board.* Minneapolis: Dennison, 1963.

Anderson, Paul S. *Storytelling with the Flannel Board Book 2.* Minneapolis: Dennison, 1970.

Bay, Jeanette Graham. *The Treasury of Flannelboard Stories.* Fort Atkinson, WI: Alleyside, 1995.

Byrd, Susannah Mississippi. *Using a Bilingual Storybook in the Classroom: A Teacher's Guide to Tell Me a Cuento/Cuentame un Story.* El Paso, TX: Cinco Puntos, 1998.

Catron, Carol Elaine, and Barbara Catron Parks. *Super Story Telling.* Minneapolis: Dennison, 1986.

Hicks, Doris Lynn. *Flannelboard Classic Tales.* Chicago: ALA, 1997.

Sierra, Judy. *Multicultural Folktales for the Feltboard and Readers' Theater.* Phoenix, AZ: Oryx, 1996.

Sierra, Judy, and Robert Kaminski. *Multicultural Folktales: Stories to Tell Young Children.* Phoenix, AZ: Oryx, 1991.

Taylor, Frances S., and Gloria G. Vaughn. *The Flannel Board Storybook.* Atlanta, GA: Humanities Unlimited, 1986.

Vonk, Idalee. *Storytelling with the Flannel Board Book Three.* Minneapolis: Dennison, 1983.

Weissman, Annie. *Transforming Storytimes into Reading and Writing Lessons.* Worthington, OH: Linworth, 2001.

Board Patterns for "Henny Penny"
Drawn by Susan Bailyn

chicken

rooster

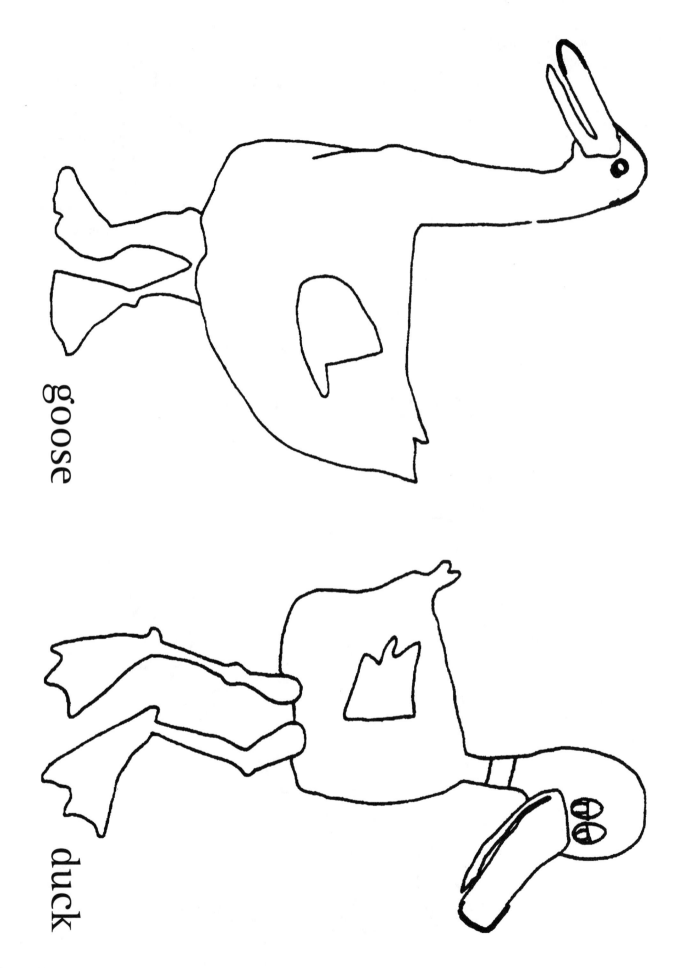

goose

duck

fox

turkey

chicken

dog

pig

bread

cat

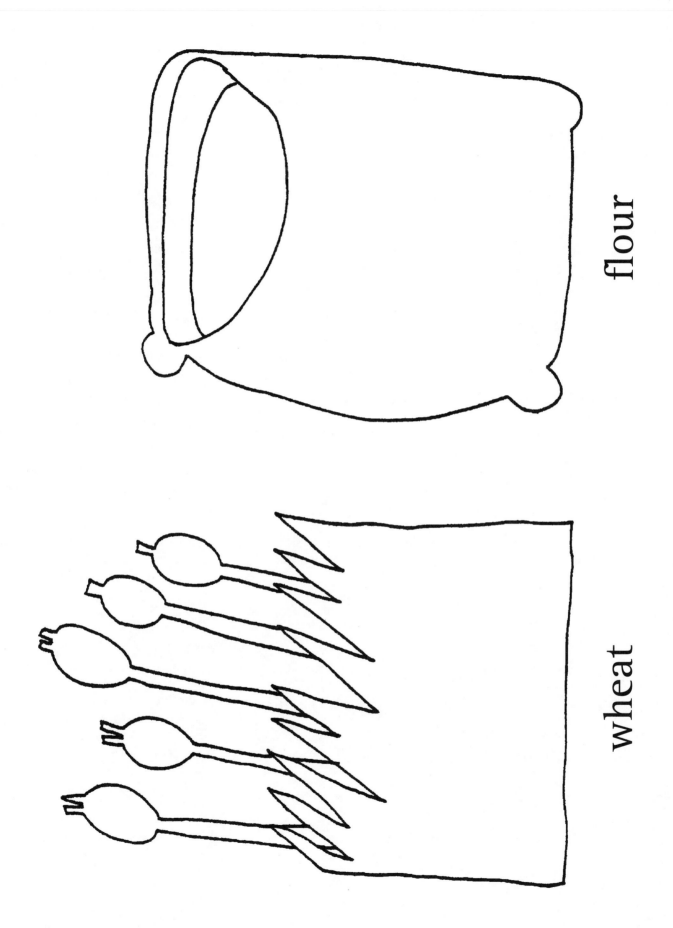

flour

wheat

Chapter 7 Getting Students into Storytelling

WHY INVOLVE STUDENTS IN STORYTELLING?

There are many educational reasons to get students into storytelling: to become intimate with the narrative form, to develop public speaking skills, to develop the reading comprehension skills of sequencing of action and oral interpretation of literature, and so on. It's also fun, and a departure from the more serious side of school. Some students will embrace this ancient art; others will be wary. For older students, consider starting with the chapter on proverbs. This gives the students a way to glide into speaking in front of a group. For younger students, teach the lessons in Chapter 5 with creative dramatics. This will introduce students in a non-threatening way to folktales and to presenting stories to an audience.

After these initial forays, the next step can be board storytelling. Start with a very familiar folktale, like "Henny Penny" or "The Little Red Hen." Then graduate to less well-known tales.

STUDENT STORYTELLING WEB SITES

There are several useful Web sites for student storytellers. The Kids' Storytelling Club is at <http://www.storycraft.com/files/welcome.htm>. The National Storytelling Network sponsors the Youth

Olympics (of storytelling). For information go to its site, <http://www.storynet.org>. Voices Across America Youth Storytelling is at <http://members.cnetech.com/kctells/>. A site for teachers with lesson plans is Storytelling in the Classroom at <http://www.storyarts.org/classroom/>.

BOARD STORIES

Note: Before this lesson, have the students cut and color the figures for either "Henny Penny" or "The Little Red Hen." The patterns are in Chapter 6. Have the students number the figures in the sequence they come in the story. Have the students put the felt tape (or magnets) on the back of each figure. Put each set of figures in a zipper bag to prevent loss. An alternative is to have parent, student, or community volunteers make a classroom set of these figures for the instructor to keep from year to year.

LESSON PLANS	*Board Storytelling Lesson 1*

Review

Say, "We recited proverbs and riddles (or acted out "Henny Penny" and "The Little Red Hen"). Now you're going to learn how to tell a folktale using a board and figures."

Objective

Students will be able to tell "Henny Penny" (or "The Little Red Hen") using the figures provided.

Whole Group Direct Instruction

Model the telling of the chosen story, either "Henny Penny" or "The Little Red Hen." Tell the story a second time, asking the audience to participate in the refrains. Before telling the story a second time, give the students tips for telling a board story, and have them raise their hands when they see you do one of the tips.

The tips are:

1. If you're nervous, breathe in and out slowly and curl and uncurl your toes.
2. Always face your audience and look the members in the eye.
3. Always speak loudly enough for everyone to hear.
4. Always speak with expression.
5. Put the figure on the board, and then look at your audience. Don't tell the story to the board!

Guided Practice

Tell the students that they are going to practice telling the same story. Split the students into pairs, giving each pair a set of figures for the story and a board. They are to practice telling the same story, except they will be using a much softer voice. Scatter the pairs around the room and monitor the pairs.

Closure

Bring the students back to the story area and have them chorally tell the story with you, as you put the figures on the board.

Note: Photocopy the figures for the stories and the text for the students. Make the figures either in the classroom or the library. Students should put their names on the back of each of their figures before putting them in the zipper bags. The recordings are for oral learners, students who do not read well, or English language learners.

Board Storytelling Lesson 2

Review

Remind students of the story they told during the previous lesson.

Objective

Students will choose a story to tell from the ones presented.

Whole Group Direct Instruction

Tell three or four easy board stories. A list of sources is at the end of this chapter. Remind students of the tips before you tell the stories, and tell them they will be choosing a story to tell from the ones they hear. Record the stories as you tell them, or beforehand, on an audiocassette or CD.

Closure

Have students choose which story they will learn.

Note: Repeat Lesson 3 as many times as necessary for the students to become proficient.

Board Storytelling Lesson 3

Review

Review the tips for board storytelling.

Objective

Students will practice telling their flannelboard stories, with feedback from their partner, the classroom teacher, and the teacher-librarian.

Whole Group Direct Instruction

Tell each of the stories one more time to the group. Tell them they will be practicing with a partner and that the listening partner's job is to keep in mind the tips and to help the teller. Tell students that they will then switch roles.

Guided Practice

Assign partners based on who's telling the same story. Have the partners practice their stories, scattered around the library.

Closure

Ask the students to tell what their partners were doing right.

It is important to keep the "audience" for the beginning storytellers very small. Pair up the storytellers with a class of younger students. Have at least six to eight boards placed around the library. After the students have practiced the stories in their classrooms, have a "dress rehearsal" in the library. Put the students into groups so that there are a variety of stories in each group. This may not always be possible, as some tales are much more popular than others and students should have a completely free choice of the story they learn. Fortunately, students in kindergarten, first grade, and second grade love hearing the same story over and over.

The third step in teaching storytelling to students is for them to choose a *short* story to tell traditionally, without any props or aids. The instructor should have veto power over the choice of story. Students do not have the experience to know which stories are difficult to learn or difficult to deliver. Consider using the stories in this book for the students' first experiences. They are guaranteed to work, although the myths may be harder to deliver than the other stories.

Again, the audience for the initial telling should be kept small, like for the board storytelling. Once the students are comfortable telling the story in front of a group of seven or eight people, increase the audience to fifteen by inviting another class to hear the stories, but split the groups between the classroom and the library, so the telling can be simultaneous. Some students may opt out at this point and should be allowed to do so. Some students will want to move to the next level, telling stories to a whole class. Arrange for them to tell stories during their lunch period for another grade level. Those who are still avid tellers after this are ready for a storytelling festival, covered in the next chapter.

LESSON PLANS

Traditional Storytelling Lesson 1

Review

Tell students that a proverb is a bit of wisdom, handed down from generation to generation.

Objective

Each student will memorize and recite a proverb in a formal manner in front of a group of ten students.

Whole Group Direct Instruction

Explain to students that this lesson is the first in a series to get them to be storytellers. Tell them that storytelling is an ancient art. Recite a proverb from Chapter 4. Tell the students to watch and listen to your presentation. They should watch your posture and expression and listen to your voice volume, pitch, and speed. Ask the students to comment on your presentation.

Guided Practice

Give the students at least one page of proverbs. Have them read the proverbs silently and pick one to memorize and perform. After the students have picked their proverbs and memorized them, pair the students so they can practice. Walk around, monitoring the practice. Make sure each student stands up and practices presenting the proverb formally.

Independent Practice

Divide the students into groups of ten. Have the students recite their proverbs in front of the group. Make sure they stand in a formal position and speak loudly enough for the group to hear easily.

Closure

Ask the students if it was easy or hard to learn and say the proverb.

Traditional Storytelling Lesson 2

Review

Have a few students recite the proverbs from the day before.

Objective

Each student will learn and tell a very short tale in a formal manner to a group of ten students.

Whole Group Direct Instruction

Tell a story from the "A" (shortest and easiest) group of stories in this book. Tell the students to pay attention to your presentation: your posture, expression, and voice volume, pitch, and speed. Ask the students to comment on your presentation when you have finished. Then tell the other stories you have chosen for the students. It is always easier to learn a story if you've heard someone else tell it. Explain how to learn a story using the information from Chapter 2.

Guided Practice

Give the students copies of the stories you told. Have them read the stories silently and pick one to learn and perform. After the students have picked their stories and learned them, pair the students so they can practice. Walk around, monitoring the practice, making sure that each student stands up and practices formally presenting the story.

Independent Practice

Divide the students into groups of ten. Have the students tell their stories in front of the group. Make sure they stand in a formal position and speak loudly enough for the group to hear easily.

Closure

Ask the students to list some tips to remember when learning and telling a story.

Review
Have a few students tell the stories from the day before.

Objective
Each student will learn and tell a very short tale in a formal manner to a group of ten students.

Whole Group Direct Instruction
Tell a story from the "A" or "B" group of stories in Chapter 9. Tell the students to pay attention to your presentation: your posture, expression, and voice volume, pitch, and speed. Ask the students to comment on your presentation when you have finished. Then tell the other stories you have chosen for the students. Remind them how to learn and tell a story.

Guided Practice
Give the students copies of the stories you told. Have them read the stories silently and pick one to learn and perform. After the students have picked their stories and learned them, pair the students so they can practice. Walk around, monitoring the practice, making sure that each student stands up and practices formally presenting the story.

Independent Practice
Divide the students into groups of ten. Have the students tell their stories in front of the group. Make sure they stand in a formal position and speak loudly enough for the group to hear easily.

Closure
Ask students how they felt before, during, and after telling a story.

Bibliography on Student Storytelling

Dubrovin, Vivian. *Storytelling for the Fun of It: A Handbook for Children*. Masonville, CO: Storycraft, 1994.

Hamilton, Martha, and Mitch Weiss. *Stories in My Pocket: Tales Kids Can Tell*. Golden, CO: Fulcrum, 1996.

Chapter 8 Storytelling Festivals

Storytelling festivals can be school, parent, district-wide, organizational, and community activities. It can happen only once, but be aware that many times festivals are so well received that they become annual events. Having planned young author days, young reader days, poetry writing conferences, and poetry recitation conferences, I can attest that storytelling festivals are easier to arrange and manage. A successful Storytelling Festival can have as few as three storytellers and fifty listeners, although extravaganzas with five storytelling areas and many storytellers are quite exciting, if a bit frantic.

SCHOOL STORYTELLING FESTIVALS

A festival at a school can be a showcase of teacher, teacher-librarian, and guest storytellers or the culmination of the storytelling unit the teacher-librarian has taught to several classes.

The easiest festival is one planned during the school day for specific grade levels, showcasing the storytelling talents of the teacher-librarian and several school staff members. The festival can be the kickoff event for units of storytelling within the school and can generate positive publicity within the school, district, and community. A date and a site should be chosen by the teacher-librarian and principal three months ahead of time. The teacher-librarian recruits and auditions willing storytellers from the faculty and requests a list of the stories they'd like to tell. The teacher-librarian then selects the stories to be included in the program, with an eye to which grade levels would be the most appropriate audience. Two months ahead of time, the storytellers should be informed of their participation and told what kind of microphone will be available. Invite the children's librarian from the local public library to participate if he or she is a storyteller. This makes it more of a community event. The festival should be planned far enough in advance to allow for publicity within the school, the district, and the community.

Check with the administration before inviting district curriculum coordinators, the superintendent, school board members, local business leaders, community people who have either supported the school or will be asked to do so, and the local media. Make sure notices are put in newsletters for parents. This should be done a month before the festival.

Two weeks ahead of the festival, make a program for the event, listing the storytellers in the order they will tell and their stories. Remember to have a table with individual water bottles, labeled for each storyteller. If gifts are to be provided for the storytellers, buy or make them at this time.

The seating can be in chairs or on the floor. It is best if the storytellers are on a stage or otherwise elevated so that all the listeners can see. The student audience should be reminded of expected behavior before the performance begins. The seating and stage configuration required should be given to the custodians, along with the microphone needs, a week before the festival.

After the festival, remember to thank the storytellers, both in person and with a short thank-you note. One idea is to take the storyteller's picture during his or her presentation and make it the cover of the note. Copies of the pictures can be posted on the library's bulletin board or Web site or in the office. It's also nice if a token gift is given to each teller after the performance.

A guest storyteller can elevate the festival to an "event." Storytelling directories are available through many state arts commissions, for which the storytellers audition. Other storyteller directories are available on the Internet at <http://www.eduscapes.com/42explore/story.htm> and <http://www.storyteller.net>. The latter site also has information about storytelling festivals all over the country. These guest storytellers charge fees, so check the budget. Money for these fees is often available through parent organizations, student councils, Title I, or Johnson O'Malley (Indian Education) funds.

Another way to present the festival is to have it be the culminating activity for storytelling units. Check out <http://www.sbac.edu/~talbot/JCF_story.html>, the Web site of W. S. Talbot Elementary School, which participated in a storytelling festival. If several classes have completed the units, call for auditions and choose the best ten storytellers to be interspersed with the teacher-librarian, staff, local public children's librarian, or professional storyteller. There can be two or three sites within the school for the festival, with specific classes invited to each site and storytellers assigned to each. This makes the audience less daunting to student storytellers. Thank-you notes and token gifts should be given to the student storytellers. School storytelling festivals can also be planned for the evenings, when more parents can attend. The following time line can be used to plan your event.

- Six months ahead of the festival, meet with the teachers to plan the units and the exact date of the festival, remembering to obtain permission from the principal. This is also the time to arrange for a professional storyteller, if one is desired.
- Three months ahead of time, teach the storytelling units. Choose the best tellers for the festival.
- A month ahead of time, order ribbons or certificates for the storytellers. This is also the time to plan the press releases with the permission and assistance of the principal and district personnel. Publicize the event in the school newsletter and marquee. Decide which classes will be invited for the audience.
- Two weeks ahead of time, have the students write invitations to their parents. Write the invitations to the school and district "dignitaries." Arrange for the space and give the room arrangements and audiovisual needs to the custodians. Ask

someone to videotape the performances, and obtain permission from parents to do this. Make up the program and schedule.

DISTRICT-WIDE STORYTELLING FESTIVALS

District-wide storytelling festivals are more complex to organize successfully, but can have a much wider range of influence. It's best to coordinate such an all-day venture through an established group, such as the district's teacher-librarians. A committee can be formed, a chair chosen, and assignments made.

- One person needs to be in charge of physical arrangements: the place (usually one of the schools), the sites for storytelling at the place, lunch, and student transportation to the site.
- Another person is responsible for the program. This includes having each teacher-librarian audition and choose the best student storytellers in each school. The number of storytellers depends on the number of schools in the district. A small district will have more storytellers per school. Each teacher-librarian is responsible for sending the names of the storytellers and the stories that will be told. The storytellers are arranged by grade level or groups of grade levels, depending on the number. The program person on the committee arranges the final program and arranges for its printing.
- Another committee person is in charge of publicity, name tags, and invitations. The out-of-district publicity needs to be channeled through the administration before sending out press and media releases. Special invitations should be sent to the parents of the storytellers, administrators, local business people, and the larger educational community.
- Another person should be in charge of contacting and arranging for a professional storyteller to present a program to the student storytellers. This person can also arrange for ribbons for the storytellers that have "Official Storyteller, Storytelling Festival," the school district's name, and the date printed on them.

SAMPLE SCHEDULE FOR DISTRICT-WIDE STORYTELLING FESTIVAL

8:00–8:30	Students are transported from their home schools to the site of the festival.
8:30–9:00	Registration and check-in. Students receive their ribbons and name tags.
9:00–10:00	First storytelling session. Half of the participants tell their stories to each other and invited classes from the hosting school. Grades 1–2 in room 7 Grades 3–4 in room 9 Grades 5–6 in room 11 Grades 7–8 in room 12 Grades 9–12 in the library
10:00–10:20	Break. Bathrooms, crackers, and water or juice should be available for storytellers.
10:30–11:30	Second storytelling session. The other half of the participants tell their stories to each other and invited classes from the hosting school. Grades 1–2 in room 7 Grades 3–4 in room 9 Grades 5–6 in room 11 Grades 7–8 in room 12 Grades 9–12 in the library
11:30–12:15	Lunch in the cafeteria or otherwise arranged.
12:30–1:15	Professional storytellers' presentation in the library or auditorium for the student storytellers, their parents, and some classes invited from the hosting school.
1:15–1:45	Student storytellers are transported back to their home schools.
	The first storytelling festival is the hardest to implement. Make sure you keep samples of all the publicity, invitations, and so on, so the next festival will be much easier to plan.

STORYTELLING EVENTS AT CONFERENCES

I've had the pleasure to coordinate several storytelling events for the Arizona Library Association. Although one was a performance by Jackie Torrance, others were events where Arizona librarians, from both public and school libraries, performed.

The first thing to do is to find out who's in charge of the conference and when program proposals are due. Before submitting a proposal, informally ask librarians, whom you or a trusted colleague has heard tell stories well, if they would be interested in performing. Remember to consult the local community colleges and universities. For example, South Mountain Community College in Phoenix has a vibrant storytelling program. Librarians must agree to speak for free as there is usually no fee given for people who are eligible to belong to the state library association. Others may be offered a small honorarium if that is allowed by the library association.

Make sure to fill out the official conference proposal sheet and to request microphones, both lavaliere and standing/detachable ones.

After the conference proposal is approved, the program committee member will tell you how much time is allotted for the storytelling event. Divide the time among the storytellers so you can allot each storyteller time for stories. Subtract a minute or two as storytellers usually run over their time. Now contact the storytellers by phone or e-mail. Let them know the time, date, and place of the event. Find out the story or stories they plan to tell. Write down the books from which the stories are taken, if they are known. Follow up with letters to the storytellers thanking them for agreeing to perform and including the pertinent information, as well as a reminder as to what story or stories they said they would tell.

You will want to make reminder phone calls or send e-mails two months, one month, two weeks, and a few days before the event. This may seem like overkill, but it will alert you to anyone who may have a problem with his or her health, getting time off work, moving, and so on.

A week before, make up a one-page program listing the storytellers, where they work or contact information, and the stories that they will tell, including the references if known. Make more copies than will be needed. People attending often take several to share with colleagues. This is good "advertising" for the storytellers, some of whom may tell stories as a side job.

Be prepared to be the master of ceremonies. Make sure you can pronounce the storytellers' names and stories correctly. Reserve the first row of chairs for the storytellers. Ask a friend to hand out the programs so you can concentrate on greeting the storytellers.

The week after the program write thank-you notes to the storytellers, thanking them for their participation and complimenting them on their storytelling.

Chapter 9   The Stories

The stories included in this section are all in the public domain. I have told them so many times that these are the distillations of my versions of the stories. The "A" section has the easiest tales. The "B" section has ones that are a little longer. The "C" section has the longest tales, but they are not necessarily the hardest to learn.

Aesop's Fables
Retold by Annie Weissman

The Wolf and the Lamb

Once a Wolf found a Lamb who had wandered away from his flock. The Wolf wanted to eat the lamb, but he also wanted to justify why he was eating the Lamb.

"Lamb, last year you insulted me!" said the Wolf.

"Wolf, I wasn't yet born then," bleated the Lamb.

"You have eaten the grass from my pasture!" said the Wolf.

"No, sir," said the Lamb, "I have not yet tasted grass."

"You drank from my well!" said the Wolf.

"No, sir," said the Lamb, "I have never tasted water. My mother's milk is still the only food and drink I have."

"I'm not going to remain hungry just because you can answer all of my arguments," said the Wolf.

He pounced on the Lamb and ate him up.

Moral: A tyrant will always find a reason for his tyranny.

The Rooster and the Jewel

One day, when a Rooster was scratching for some food for himself and his hens, he found a large jewel. He looked at it but did not pick it up.

"If the Farmer had found this," the Rooster said, "he would have taken it home and kept it as one of his most precious possessions. But I have found it and have no use for it. I would rather have one piece of corn than all the jewels in the world."

Moral: One person's junk is another person's treasure.

The Dog and His Shadow

A Dog with a piece of meat in his mouth was crossing a river on a bridge. He saw his own shadow in the water and thought it was another dog, with a piece of meat twice the size of his own. The Dog let go of his own meat and attacked the other dog to get the bigger piece of meat. But he lost both: the one which he grasped at in the water, for it was only a shadow, and his own, because it had already traveled downstream and out of sight.

Moral: Greed can make you lose what you already have.

The Farmer and the Snake

One winter a Farmer found a Snake that was stiff and frozen. He felt sorry for the Snake. He picked it up and placed it under his clothing, next to his skin. The warmth from the Farmer's body revived the Snake. The Snake, following his natural instincts, bit the Farmer.

"Oh," cried the Farmer with his dying breath, "I am rightly rewarded for helping a scoundrel."

Moral: The greatest kindnesses will not change the ungrateful.

The Donkey, the Fox, and the Lion

The Donkey and the Fox made a pact to protect each other before they went out into the forest to hunt. They had not gone far when they met a Lion.

The Fox, who saw the immediate danger, talked quietly to the Lion. He promised to help the Lion capture the Donkey if the Lion would promise not to hurt the Fox.

Then the Fox, after telling the Donkey there was no danger, led the Donkey into a deep pit. The Donkey fell in.

When the Lion saw that the Donkey was trapped, he attacked and ate the Fox. He could wait and eat the Donkey later, whenever he wanted.

Moral: Those who betray others may themselves be betrayed.

The Fox and the Crow

A Crow stole some meat. She flew back to a branch and held the meat in her beak. The Fox saw this and wanted the meat for himself. He thought of a plan to get it.

"Crow, you are so handsome! Your shape is perfect. Your complexion is beautiful. If only your voice was as pretty as your body, you would deserve to be the Queen of the Birds."

The Crow, anxious to show that her voice was as beautiful as her body, cawed loudly. When she did this, the meat dropped from her beak and fell into the Fox's mouth.

The Fox licked his lips and said, "My dear Crow, your voice is fine, but you're not very clever."

Moral: Beware of flatterers.

The Fox and the Goat

One day a Fox slipped into a well from which he couldn't get out. Soon a Goat came to the same well to get a drink. He saw the Fox in the well and asked him if the water was good.

The Fox did not tell the Goat he couldn't get out, but said happily "The water is delicious! It's the best water I've ever had! Come down here and taste it!"

The Goat thought only of his thirst and jumped down the well. As he was drinking, the Fox told the Goat of their problem of being stuck in the well.

"I have an idea," said the Fox. "If you will put your front feet on the wall of the well and bend your head, I will run up your back and get out of the well. Then I will help you get out."

The Goat easily agreed. The Fox climbed on the Goat's back and safely reached the mouth of the well. As soon as he was out of the well, the Fox started to run away.

"You were supposed to help me get out!" the Goat called after the Fox. "You broke your promise!"

The Fox turned around and said, "You are so foolish! If you had as many brains in your head as you have hairs in your beard, you would never have gone into the well before you saw whether there was a way up. If you had, you would have seen there was no way to escape."

Moral: Look before you leap.

The Fox and the Grapes

A hungry Fox saw some clusters of ripe grapes hanging from a vine that grew on a trellis. She jumped and tried all of her tricks to get the grapes. She got very tired but she could not reach the grapes. At last she turned away. To hide her disappointment she said, "Those grapes are not as ripe as I thought. They are sour, so I don't want them anyway."

Moral: It's easy to hate what you cannot get.

The Wolf in Sheep's Clothing

Once a Wolf decided to disguise himself in order to get some food without having to chase it. He put on the skin of a sheep, found a flock of sheep in a pasture, and hid among them. The shepherd did not see him.

In the evening, the Wolf was herded back to a farm and shut up in a pen with the sheep. He looked forward to a feast of sheep that night.

But the shepherd wanted some meat for his dinner. He mistook the Wolf for a sheep and killed him.

Moral: If you go looking to harm someone, you will find harm yourself.

The Crab and Its Mother

A Crab said to her son, "Why do you walk so much to one side? You would look much better if you walked straight forward."

The young Crab replied, "That's probably true, Mother. If you show me how to walk the straight way, I will promise to do that."

The Mother tried and tried to walk straight, but she couldn't.

"If you can't do it," said the young Crab, "don't expect me to be able to do it."

Moral: Example is a more powerful teacher than talking.

Fables of Jean De La Fontaine
Retold by Annie Weissman

The North Wind and the Sun

Once upon a time the North Wind and the Sun were arguing over who was stronger.

"I can make the trees bend to the ground," bragged the North Wind.

Below them, a traveler was crossing the plain on his horse.

"See that traveler?" the Sun said. "I wonder which of us could make him take off his coat?"

"I'll show you once and for all how strong I am," the North Wind said. "Let's set ourselves to the task. Let us agree that whoever can get the traveler to take off his coat is the stronger of us."

"I'll agree to that," replied the Sun. "You may try first."

The Sun went behind a cloud.

The North Wind blew and blew and blew.

The North Wind's icy blasts chilled the traveler, making him clutch his coat closer to his body.

After many tries, the North Wind stopped his blowing.

The Sun came out and shone his warmth at the traveler. He became warm in the direct sun and took off his coat.

Moral: The Sun was able to accomplish with gentle warmth what the North Wind could not, despite all his harshness.

The Fly and the Ant

Once a Fly and an Ant were arguing over who was better.

The fly boasted, "You think you are as good as me? I fly! I can go to the palace and sit on the royal table. I can eat food that is better than anything you eat. You have to slave three days to drag home a little bit of something to eat. I can sit on the head of a king, an emperor, or a pretty girl. I can kiss her lips or play in her hair."

"You do go to the palace," said the Ant, "but so can anyone. You are treated as a pest and hated. It doesn't matter that you can serve yourself first for food. It doesn't taste better whether you eat first or last. Yes, you can land on the king's head, but you may be killed for doing that. Although you can fly, you are called a parasite. Stop your bragging. Flies in the court are shooed out.

"When the times are hard, you will die of hunger and cold. I will enjoy the fruit of my labor. I won't have to go looking for food in the cold or rain. I have stored provisions in a safe place so I won't have to worry. I don't just talk, I plan for the future. Therefore, my life is better than yours."

Moral: Work steadily, and always plan for the hard times.

Another Tale

A Danish folktale retold in Southwestern style by Annie Weissman

Two Ranching Families

Once there were two ranch families who lived on each side of a mesa.

One family had three girls. The oldest girl's name was Lin. The middle daughter's name was Lin Lin-er-rin. The youngest daughter's name was Lin Lin-er-rin Lupe Linning-grin.

On the other side of the mesa was a family of boys. The oldest boy's name was Dan. The middle son's name was Dan Dan-dee-ran. The youngest boy's name was Dan Dan-dee-ran Danning Fan.

The two families met and the appropriate young men and women fell in love. Lin married Dan. Lin Lin-er-rin married Dan Dan-dee-ran. And Lin Lin-er-in Lupe Linning-grin married Dan Dan-dee-ran Danning Fan. Wasn't that grand!

Anansi and the Two Weddings
An Ashanti tale from West Africa retold by Annie Weissman

One time, Anansi, the clever but greedy spider, received an invitation to a wedding for the following Saturday in a town to the east. The bride was the daughter of a rich man.

"What a wonderful feast there will be!" thought Anansi. It made him hungry to think of the eggplant salad, goat soup, and banana cake.

The next day he received an invitation to another wedding for the same day, this time in a town to the west. The bride's father was also very rich and known to give a good party. There would be plantain fufu, fish-ball stew, and fried yams.

"Which shall I attend?" Anansi asked himself. He knew each feast would be one to remember in leaner times.

Then Anansi got an idea. He could attend both dinners if he were clever about it. On Saturday he tied two ropes around his waist. The first he gave to a friend who was attending the wedding in the town to the east.

"When it is time to sit down for the big dinner, tug on this rope and I'll come right away," Anansi told his friend.

The second rope he gave to another friend who was attending the wedding in the town to the west.

"When it is time to sit down for the big dinner, tug on this rope and I'll come right away," Anansi told his friend.

Anansi sat, dreaming of good things to eat and getting impatient.

Finally there was a tug on the rope that led to the town in the west. But before Anansi could take off the ropes, his friend who went to the wedding in the town to the east started pulling on the rope.

The ropes squeezed Anansi, each pulling him in opposite directions. They pulled tauter and tauter around Anansi's waist. His waist got thinner and thinner. He did not go to either wedding feast.

And spiders' waists remain thin to this very day.

One Good Deed Deserves Another
A Mexican tale retold by Annie Weissman

Once upon a time, a ranch hand named Paco was walking through the desert at the edge of town. He saw a rattlesnake caught under a rock.

"Pleasssse, Missssster Man. Pleasssse take this sssssstone off my back. If you don't, I will die."

Paco was a kindly soul, so he lifted the heavy rock off the snake. As soon as he did, the rattlesnake coiled and rattled his tail, ready to strike.

"Wait!" said Paco. "I just saved your life and you're going to kill me? Doesn't one good deed deserve another?"

"Who told you such trash?" asked the snake. "In the animal world, it's eat or be eaten."

"I think the world is a good place where people treat each other kindly," said Paco.

"I'll give you a chance," said the snake. "We'll ask the next three to go by whether one good deed deserves another. If even one agrees with you, I'll spare you."

The first to come by was a chicken. Paco told him of the situation.

"I laid eggs my whole life for the farmer. Now that I can't lay eggs, he's going to put me in the Sunday cooking pot. In my life, one good deed does not lead to another."

"One for me!" said the snake as the chicken went on her way.

The next to come by was a donkey. Paco told him the story of what had happened between him and the snake.

"I agree with the snake," said the donkey. "I worked hard hauling things for my owner. Now that I am too old to carry anything, he is selling me for slaughter."

"That's two that agree with me!" said the snake. "Only one more chance for you."

The next to come along was a coyote. He listened very carefully as Paco told him about lifting the stone from the snake and the snake's wanting to bite and kill him.

The coyote thought for a while.

"I really need to see the situation as it was," said the coyote.

"All right," said the snake.

Paco put the large stone back on the rattlesnake's back.

"Can you move?" asked the coyote.

"No, it is just as before," said the snake.

"Then it really doesn't matter what I think," said the coyote.

The coyote and Paco went down the road for lunch.

The Teeny Tiny Woman
An English folktale retold by Annie Weissman

Once upon a time there lived a teeny tiny woman in a teeny tiny house in a teeny tiny town.

One day the teeny tiny woman was a teeny tiny bit bored, so she decided to take a teeny tiny walk in the teeny tiny town. She put on her teeny tiny bonnet and went out the teeny tiny door of her teeny tiny house.

The teeny tiny woman had gone a teeny tiny way when she saw a teeny tiny gate to a teeny tiny graveyard. The teeny tiny woman went through the teeny tiny gate and saw a teeny tiny bone on a teeny tiny grave.

The teeny tiny woman thought, "That teeny tiny bone will make some teeny tiny soup for my teeny tiny supper!"

The teeny tiny woman took the teeny tiny bone, put it in her teeny tiny pocket, and went back on her teeny tiny walk. After a teeny tiny time, the teeny tiny woman was a teeny tiny bit tired, so she went back to her teeny tiny house.

She went up the teeny tiny stairs to her teeny tiny room. She took off her teeny tiny bonnet and hung it up on the teeny tiny hat rack. She took the teeny tiny bone from her teeny tiny pocket and put it in the teeny tiny cupboard. Then she got into her teeny tiny bed for a teeny tiny nap.

But after a teeny tiny time, the teeny tiny woman heard a teeny tiny voice from the teeny tiny cupboard.

"Who took my bo-o-o-one?"

The teeny tiny woman was a teeny tiny bit frightened. She pulled the teeny tiny covers over her teeny tiny head and went back to her teeny tiny nap.

But a teeny tiny time later, the teeny tiny woman heard a teeny tiny voice from the teeny tiny cupboard saying a teeny tiny bit louder:

"Who took my bo-o-o-one?"

The teeny tiny woman was a teeny tiny bit more frightened. She pulled the teeny tiny covers a teeny tiny bit further over her teeny tiny head and went back to her teeny tiny nap.

But a teeny tiny time later, the teeny tiny woman heard a teeny tiny voice from the teeny tiny cupboard saying a teeny tiny bit louder:

"Who took my **bone**?"

The teeny tiny woman was a teeny tiny bit more frightened, but she pulled the teeny tiny covers from her teeny tiny head, and she said in her loudest teeny tiny voice, **"Take it!"**

And that's the story of the teeny tiny woman.

The Three Wishes

A German folktale retold by Annie Weissman

Once upon a time there was a poor woodcutter who lived with his wife in a tiny cottage at the edge of the forest.

One afternoon, as he was in the middle of the forest, he got ready to chop down a tree that had been hit by lightning.

"Please!" cried a squeaky voice. "Please, don't cut this tree!"

"Who are you?" asked the woodcutter.

"I'm a wood nymph," answered the voice.

"If this is your home," said the woodcutter, "I'll cut down a different tree."

"I will reward you for your kindness," said the squeaky voice. "I will grant you three wishes."

"Three wishes!" exclaimed the woodcutter. "I must go home and consult my wife."

The woodcutter ran home and told his wife about the wood nymph and the three wishes. "What shall we wish for?" he asked.

He and his wife traded suggestions for hours with no agreement. Should they wish for money, a new home, new clothes, or a farm?

The woodcutter's stomach growled.

"I'm hungry. I wish I had a sweet, fat, sausage to eat."

As soon as the words were out of his mouth, a fat, juicy, piping hot, sweet sausage appeared on the table.

"You idiot!" shouted his wife. "You have wasted one of our wishes on a sausage! I wish that sausage was on the end of your nose!"

As soon as the words were out of her mouth, the sausage came off the plate and attached itself to the end of the woodcutter's nose.

"Oh no!" he cried. "You wasted another wish!"

His wife laughed. He looked ridiculous with a sausage on the end of his nose.

"We still have one wish left," she said. "Should we wish for bags of gold?"

"What good will bags of gold do me if I have to live for the rest of my life with a sausage at the end of my nose?"

They argued for a short time, but finally they agreed.

"I wish the sausage was back on the plate," said the woodcutter.

The sausage fell off the woodcutter's nose and back onto the plate.

The woodcutter and his wife ate the sausage for dinner. And it was tasty!

Pecos Bill

An American tall tale retold by Annie Weissman

Once there lived a family with 15 children. The youngest one, just a baby, was Bill. The family set out on a wagon train west. One day, near the Pecos River in Texas, the children started to fight. Bill got knocked out of the wagon. No one noticed until that evening, when it was too late to find him.

Bill was raised by coyotes for the next 15 years. Then a cowboy saw him behind a bush. Bill told the cowboy he was a coyote, but the cowboy pointed out that Bill didn't have a tail. Pecos Bill decided that if he wasn't a coyote, he'd be a cowboy.

One time, on his way across Texas, his horse stepped in a hole and couldn't walk, so Pecos Bill had to carry him. After he'd walked 100 miles, a rattlesnake started rattling, but Pecos Bill just smacked it so it couldn't bite him and tossed it around his neck. After another hundred miles, a mountain lion appeared. Pecos Bill called him a mangy housecat. That angered the mountain lion so much that he attacked. But Pecos Bill got him into a headlock and squeezed so hard, the mountain lion cried. Then Pecos Bill took the saddle off his horse, put it on the mountain lion, and rode him to his ranch. The pasture of his ranch was all of Arizona. New Mexico was the corral. At the ranch he tamed the wildest bronco, named Widow Maker. That became his horse because nobody else could ride him.

One day, when Pecos Bill was letting Widow Maker drink at a river, he saw a young woman with hair all knotted and a front tooth missing. She was beautiful! He watched as she whistled and a catfish as big as a whale came to the surface. It held still while the woman put a saddle and bridle on it. She yelled, "Ride!" That catfish took her for some ride, like a bucking bronco, but the woman held on.

"That's my type of gal," thought Pecos Bill.

When she was done with her ride, he asked her name.

"I'm Slue-Foot Sue," she said.

They fell in love and got married. For the wedding Slue-Foot Sue got all dolled up and wore a bustle under her dress. After the wedding, Slue-Foot Sue asked Pecos Bill for a favor.

"Anything you want, Sue," he promised.

"I want to ride on Widow Maker," she said.

Now, Pecos Bill had to let her, because he had promised.

Widow Maker snorted as Sue got on his back. He bucked so hard that he bounced Sue into the sky. When she came down, she landed on her bustle. It acted like a spring and she bounced up even higher. Pecos Bill had to get out his rope and lasso her down.

After that they settled down on a ranch they built near the Pecos River.

Paul Bunyan

An American tall tale retold by Annie Weissman

Once upon a time there lived a logger named Paul Bunyan. He was born in Maine. Although his parents were of normal size, Paul Bunyan was 100 pounds when he was born. He was so big that his parents built a floating cradle for him in the sea, right beside their house. Baby Paul rocked in his cradle so hard that he made 70-foot waves that moved Boston from Maine to Massachusetts, where it is today. Paul's family moved him to the backwoods, where Paul's father had a logging camp.

Paul grew larger each day, by several feet. Soon he was too big for a house. When he was four years old, Paul was so strong he was able to start helping his father with cutting down trees and hauling them to the mill.

One winter, the snow was blue! Paul was walking in the forest when he saw two ears sticking out from the blue snow. He pulled out a baby ox. He held the ox close to his chest to warm up the frozen animal. After a while, the calf warmed up, but it stayed blue, because of the snow. Paul brought the calf home and named her "Babe." Babe grew as fast as Paul had. She got to be as big as 42 ax handles between her eyes!

One time, Paul was logging in Minnesota. He had to get the logs down to the sawmill in New Orleans. Paul decided the best way to do this was to make a river. His cook, Hot Slim Biscuit, made Paul his usual breakfast of 20 pounds of bacon; 15 loaves of bread; 214 pancakes, each one buttered and soaked with a bottle of syrup; and 10 gallons of milk. After breakfast, Paul hooked up Babe to a plow made out of huge pine trees and dug out a river. They used to call it the Mississippi River. I think they still do.

After many years of clearing trees from the states of Iowa and Kansas, Paul Bunyan and Babe went off into the woods. They were never seen again. But loggers will tell you that when you hear thunder, it's just Paul calling to Babe. And when you hear the wind whistling through the trees, it's just Paul walking through the woods.

Escaped Maniac

An American urban legend retold by Annie Weissman

Once when I was in high school, I had a date with a college boy. His name was Frank Franco. He took me to the movies, then out to Greenwood Lake to kiss. He turned the radio to soft music, put away the console on the front seat, and moved very close to me. He kissed me softly on the lips.

Suddenly, the music was interrupted by a breaking story.

"A convicted ax murderer has escaped from the State Prison for the Insane. He is considered very dangerous. The most noticeable feature about him is the hook on the end of his left arm. If you see this man, do NOT approach him. Call 9-1-1 or the State Police immediately!"

"How creepy!" I said.

"I'll keep you safe," Frank said, as he pulled me closer and hugged me.

"Isn't that state prison near here?" I asked.

"Yeah," Frank said. "It borders the other side of this lake."

He leaned over and nibbled on my ear.

I sat up straight and said, "I'm not comfortable being here, Frank. Take me home."

"Come on, baby, we just got here. I'll protect you."

Frank planted a big wet one on my lips. I kissed him back.

I heard a scratching at my door.

"Did you hear that noise on my door?" I asked.

Before Frank could answer, the scratching noise came again, louder.

"Let's get out of here!" I screamed.

Frank jumped back to his seat and put the car in reverse. With screeching tires, we sped out of the parking lot. He finally slowed down when we got into town.

"I want to go home," I said.

"The night is young. Let's go walking on the golf course."

"I'm not going anywhere but home," I insisted.

Frank scowled but drove me home. I invited him in, but he said he was going to go to the pool hall. He got out and walked to my side of the car to open the door.

Frank screamed!

My parents always waited up for me, with the porch light on. My father came running out of the house.

I got out on the driver's side since no one would open my door.

I started screaming too when I saw the hook on the door handle.

Followed Home

An American urban legend retold by Annie Weissman

When I was in high school, I used to go to the basketball games on Friday nights with my friends. I always drove myself because I lived outside of town.

One Friday night, our team was beating the team from a neighboring town badly. At halftime the score was 55 to 12. I was tired, so I said good-bye to my friends and left the gym.

I got into my car and left the parking lot. A pickup truck followed me out. I got on the highway to go home and so did the truck. I had only gone a mile or so, when the truck flashed its bright lights. That almost blinded me! I sped up to get away from the truck, but it kept pace with me. There was no traffic, so I couldn't put a car between us.

A little while later, the brights flashed again. Now I was really annoyed. I honked my horn and sped up. The other truck sped up too.

I was close to my exit when the jerk did it again, temporarily blinding me. I took my exit, but the truck followed me. Now I was getting a little frightened. I wove through the town, then turned onto the forest road that led to my house. So did the other truck!

Now I was scared. I floored my car and careened around the sharp turns. I knew this dirt road so well I figured I could lose the creep. But he stayed right behind me, and put on his brights again and again.

I pulled off the road, into my driveway. The pickup truck pulled in right after me. I honked the horn, and then I jumped out of the car and ran to the house. My mom opened the door. I ran in and slammed it shut. I ran to the phone and dialed the sheriff's department. The operator said to stay put; she'd send a deputy.

The pickup truck stayed parked in our driveway with the lights on.

Finally the deputy arrived and knocked on the door. I told him the whole story. He listened intently, then went outside. He shined his flashlight in the front seat of the pickup and then tapped it on the window. He told the guy to step out.

"I certainly will, Officer," the guy said, "but it's not me you want. It's the guy crouched down in the back seat of her car. I saw him rise up from the back seat as the young woman left the parking lot. I followed her, putting on my brights every time he got up."

The deputy walked up to my car and jerked open the back door. There was a guy, crouched on the floor, holding a knife.

The guy in the pickup truck had saved my life!

The Golden Arm

An American tale retold by Annie Weissman

Once upon a time there lived a man and a woman who fell in love and got married. Just a year after they were married, the woman was in a terrible car accident and had to have her arm amputated. The man loved her so much that he bought her a golden arm to replace the one she'd lost.

The couple lived happily for many years. Then the woman died, of natural causes.

On the day of her funeral, after the burial, the man went back to his home. He sat at the kitchen table, missing his wife. He thought about all the good times they'd had, and the hard times, too. He started to think about her golden arm. She didn't need it anymore. Gold was worth so much more now than when he had purchased the arm for her. He didn't think she'd mind.

He got up and went to the basement for a shovel. He walked through the forest, back to the cemetery. He dug up his wife's grave. When he found the coffin, he opened it up, detached the golden arm, and took it. He closed the coffin quickly. He tucked the golden arm under his own, and started back through the forest.

A storm came up. There was thunder and lightning. The wind whistled through the pines. "Whooo took my golden arm?"

"It's just the wind," the man told himself, but he walked more quickly.

A little while later, he heard something again.

"Whooo took my golden arm?"

"It's just the wind, just the wind!" he said, but he started to run.

Just as he reached his home, the wind came up again.

"Whooo took my golden arm?"

The man ran into his house, locked the door, and fastened the deadbolt.

He went upstairs and got into bed. He put the golden arm under the quilt.

He heard a tapping at the door.

"Whooo took my golden arm?"

The man shivered.

He heard someone coming up the stairs.

"Whooo took my golden arm?"

He heard someone's footsteps in the hallway.

"Whooo took my golden arm?"

He put his head under the quilt as he heard someone opening the squeaky door.

Someone stepped right next to the bed.

"Whooo took my golden arm? **YOU did!**"

La Llorona, the Weeping Woman

A Mexican tale retold by Annie Weissman

Once upon a time, in a village on the western coast of Mexico, a man was walking home late at night. The streets were dark and deserted. He walked for quite a while until he saw the most beautiful woman he had ever seen. She had long, black hair. She was dressed in a white gown that dragged on the ground.

She came up to him and whispered, "My children, my children!"

Then she turned and walked away from him. She was so beautiful he could not stand to let her out of his sight, so he followed her. His footsteps could be heard on the pavement, but she glided along, making no noise.

She led him to the ocean's edge. She glided out onto the breaking waves. He knew he should stay on the water's edge, but he couldn't bear to lose sight of her. He went into the water up to his ankles, up to his knees, then up to his waist. He followed her up to his neck. The waves pulled him under. He was never heard from again.

Another night, a month later, another man was walking home late at night. The streets were dark and deserted. He walked for quite a while until he saw the most beautiful woman he had ever seen. She had long, black hair. She was dressed in a white gown that dragged on the ground.

She came up to him and whispered, "My children, my children!"

Then she turned and walked away from him. She was so beautiful he could not stand to let her out of his sight, so he followed her. His footsteps could be heard on the pavement, but she glided along, making no noise.

She led him to the ocean's edge. She glided out onto the breaking waves.

But this man was more cautious than the other one. He called out, "Are you a ghost, or are you real? Or are you La Llorona, the Weeping Woman?"

She replied, "What does the ocean look like?"

The man screamed as blood churned from the white caps. He closed his eyes. When he opened them, the woman was gone.

La Llorona was once a beautiful but poor young lady who married a very rich man. His family disowned him and wouldn't give him any money. The couple had three children. The man got tired of being poor. He planned to take the children and return to his parents. When the woman heard of this, she went crazy. The night before he was to leave, she took her children to the river and drowned them. The next morning, she didn't remember what she had done. She went to look for her children. She searched for the rest of her life for her children. When she died, her ghost continued to search and to lure innocent people into water and to their deaths.

So, if you are by any water tonight—a lake, a pool, a pond, the ocean, or a stream—and you see a beautiful woman all dressed in white, do not go near. For you might meet La Llorona.

The Three Billy Goats Gruff
A Norwegian tale retold by Annie Weissman

Once upon a time, there lived three billy goats, and the last name of all three was Gruff. They ate grass and got fat, and they ate more grass and got fatter. But one day there was no more grass on their hillside. There was a hillside nearby, but in between the hillsides was a river. There was a bridge over the river, but underneath the bridge lived a nasty troll. He had eyes as big as saucers and a nose as long as a poker.

The first, and smallest, billy goat started across the bridge.

Trip, trap, trip, trap, went the bridge under the weight of the first Billy Goat Gruff.

"WHO'S THAT WALKING ON MY BRIDGE?" roared the troll.

"It is I, the first Billy Goat Gruff," said the smallest billy goat in his soft voice.

"I'M GOING TO EAT YOU UP!" roared the troll.

"Oh, please, don't eat me," said the first Billy Goat Gruff. "Wait for my bigger brother. He's got a lot more meat on his bones."

"All right, be off with you," said the troll.

So the first Billy Goat Gruff got across the bridge safely.

Then the second Billy Goat Gruff started across the bridge.

TRIP, trap, TRIP, trap, went the bridge under the weight of the second Billy Goat Gruff.

"WHO'S THAT WALKING ON MY BRIDGE?" roared the troll.

"It is I, the second Billy Goat Gruff," said the second Billy Goat Gruff in his middle-sized voice.

"I'M GOING TO EAT YOU UP!" roared the troll.

"Oh, please, don't eat me," said the second Billy Goat Gruff. "Wait for my bigger brother. He's got a lot more meat on his bones."

"All right, be off with you," said the troll.

So the second Billy Goat Gruff got across the bridge safely.

Then the third and the biggest Billy Goat Gruff started across the bridge. TRIP, TRAP, TRIP, TRAP! The bridge moaned and groaned under the weight of the third Billy Goat Gruff.

"WHO'S THAT WALKING ON MY BRIDGE?" roared the troll.

"It is I, the third, and biggest, Billy Goat Gruff," said the third Billy Goat Gruff in his great big voice.

"I'M GOING TO EAT YOU UP!" roared the troll.

"NO YOU WON'T!" said the third Billy Goat Gruff. "I've got two big spears, and I'll knock out your eyeballs to your ears. I've got two big stones, and I'll crush you to bits, body, and bones!"

"We'll see about that!" said the troll as he sprang up on the bridge.

The third Billy Goat Gruff lowered his head and butted the troll into a million pieces that washed down the river.

Then the third Billy Goat Gruff walked safely across the bridge.

All three Billy Goats Gruff went up the hillside and ate grass. They ate grass and got fat, and ate more grass and got fatter. And if the fat hasn't fallen off them yet, they're fat still.

Snip, snap, snout, this tale's told out.

The Wide-Mouthed Frog
Retold by Annie Weissman

Once upon a time a wide-mouthed frog lived with his wife along the banks of a slow-moving river that twisted its way around a bend. The wife was about to give birth to babies. She didn't know what to feed her babies, so she sent her husband into the world to find out.

The wide-mouthed frog hopped away from the grassy banks of the river and into the nearby woods. He came upon a mouse.

"Hello!" said the wide-mouthed frog. "I'm a wide-mouthed frog."

"Hello," said the mouse. "I'm a mouse."

"My wife is going to have babies soon, and we need to know what to feed them. What do you feed your babies?"

"We feed our babies grain and cheese that we steal from barns."

"That doesn't sound tasty for a wide-mouthed frog, but thank you for the information."

The wide-mouthed frog wandered further into the underbrush, where he encountered an orange, black, and yellow patterned corn snake.

"Hello!" said the wide-mouthed frog. "I'm a wide-mouthed frog."

"Hello," said the snake. "I'm a snake."

"My wife is going to have babies soon, and we need to know what to feed them. What do you feed your babies?"

"We feed our babies eggs that we steal from nests."

"That doesn't sound tasty for a wide-mouthed frog, but thank you for the information."

The wide-mouthed frog was meandering further in the woods when he saw a huge shadow overhead. All of sudden, an owl swooped down in front of him.

"Hello!" said the wide-mouthed frog. "I'm a wide-mouthed frog."

"Hello," said the owl. "I'm an owl."

"My wife is going to have babies soon, and we need to know what to feed them. What do you feed your babies?"

"We feed our babies live mice that we catch. We swallow them whole and then spit out the bones."

"That doesn't sound tasty for a wide-mouthed frog, but thank you for the information."

The wide-mouthed frog wandered further into the forest. He heard a cry from above. He looked up at an animal lying on a branch.

"Hello!" said the wide-mouthed frog. "I'm a wide-mouthed frog."

"Hello," said the bobcat. "I'm a bobcat."

"My wife is going to have babies soon, and we need to know what to feed them. What do you feed your babies?"

"We feed our babies raw red meat that we chomp on."

"That doesn't sound tasty for a wide-mouthed frog, but thank you for the information."

The wide-mouthed frog came to a swamp. It wasn't like his clear, clean river. It was muddy and he couldn't see the bottom. He saw two eyes open from what he thought was a floating log. This scared the frog.

"Hello," said the wide-mouthed frog timidly.

"Hello," said the animal.

"What kind of animal are you?" asked the wide-mouthed frog.

"I'm an alligator," said the alligator.

"My wife is going to have babies soon, and we need to know what to feed them. What do you feed your babies?"

"We feed our babies wide-mouthed frogs," said the alligator.

The wide-mouthed frog opened his mouth only a little way, hiding its wideness. His voice sounded muffled when he spoke.

"That doesn't sound tasty, but thank you for the information."

The wide-mouthed frog turned and hopped as far away as he could, just ahead of the alligator's jaws. He hopped through the forest and around the bend to the grassy banks of his clear, clean river. And he and his wife decided to feed their favorite treat to their babies: sweet, tasty flies.

Henny Penny

Retold by Annie Weissman

Once upon a time, there lived a chicken named Henny Penny. One day, as she was pecking for some food, an acorn fell on her head.

"Oh my! Oh my! The sky is falling! I must go and tell the king."

She went along the road until she met her frend, a rooster named Cocky Locky.

"Where are you going, Henny Penny?"

"I am going to the king, to tell him that the sky is falling."

"May I go too?" asked Cocky Locky.

"Certainly," said Henny Penny.

So Henny Penny and Cocky Locky went off to see the king.

They walked along and walked along until they saw another friend. It was a duck named Ducky Lucky.

"Where are you going, Henny Penny and Cocky Locky?"

"We are going to the king, to tell him that the sky is falling."

"May I go too?" asked Ducky Lucky.

"Certainly," said Henny Penny.

So Henny Penny, Cocky Locky, and Ducky Lucky went off to see the king.

They walked along and walked along until they saw another friend. It was a goose named Goosey Lucy.

"Where are you going, Henny Penny, Cocky Locky, and Ducky Lucky?"

"We are going to the king, to tell him that the sky is falling."

"May I go too?" asked Goosey Lucy.

"Certainly," said Henny Penny.

So Henny Penny, Cocky Locky, Ducky Lucky, and Goosey Lucy all went off to see the king.

They walked along and walked along until they saw another friend. It was a turkey named Turkey Lurkey.

"Where are you going, Henny Penny, Cocky Locky, Ducky Lucky, and Goosey Lucy?"

"We are going to the king, to tell him that the sky is falling."

"May I go too?" asked Turkey Lurkey.

"Certainly," said Henny Penny.

So Henny Penny, Cocky Locky, Ducky Lucky, Goosey Lucy, and Turkey Lurkey all went off to see the king.

They walked along and walked along until they saw someone who was not their friend. It was a red fox named Foxy Loxy.

"Where are you going, Henny Penny, Cocky Locky, Ducky Lucky, Goosey Lucy, and Turkey Lurkey?" asked Foxy Loxy as he licked his lips.

"We are going to the king, to tell him that the sky is falling."

"May I go too?" asked Foxy Loxy.

"Certainly," said Henny Penny.

"But you are going the wrong way," said Foxy Loxy. "Follow me. I will show you the way to the king's castle."

So Henny Penny, Cocky Locky, Ducky Lucky, Goosey Lucy, and Turkey Lurkey all followed Foxy Loxy. They followed him straight into Foxy Loxy's den, where there were five hungry little foxes waiting.

No one ever heard again from Henny Penny, Cocky Locky, Ducky Lucky, Goosey Lucy, or Turkey Lurkey. And the king never heard that the sky was falling.

The Little Red Hen

Retold by Annie Weissman

Once upon a time an industrious little red hen lived with three of her friends: a pig, a dog, and a cat. The little red hen did all the work around the house. She did all the cooking for the four of them. She washed all the dishes. She cleaned the floors. She made the beds. The pig, the dog, and the cat did no work.

One day the little red hen found a grain of wheat.

"Who will help me plant this wheat?" asked the little red hen.

"Not I!" said the pig, who went out to ooze in the mud.

"Not I!" said the dog, who went out for a snooze under the oak tree.

"Not I!" said the cat, who curled up by the fireplace.

"Then I'll do it myself!" said the little red hen. And she did.

She planted the grain of wheat. She watered and she weeded. The grain of wheat grew.

"Who will help me harvest this wheat?" asked the little red hen.

"Not I!" said the pig, who went out to ooze in the mud.

"Not I!" said the dog, who went out for a snooze under the oak tree.

"Not I!" said the cat, who curled up by the fireplace.

"Then I'll do it myself!" said the little red hen. And she did.

After she had cut down the wheat, the little red hen asked, "Who will help me take this wheat to the miller to be ground into flour?"

"Not I!" said the pig, who went out to ooze in the mud.

"Not I!" said the dog, who went out for a snooze under the oak tree.

"Not I!" said the cat, who curled up by the fireplace.

"Then I'll do it myself!" said the little red hen. And she did.

The little red hen took the wheat to the miller and had it ground into flour. When she returned home she asked, "Who will help me bake bread from this flour?"

"Not I!" said the pig, who went out to ooze in the mud.

"Not I!" said the dog, who went out for a snooze under the oak tree.

"Not I!" said the cat, who curled up by the fireplace.

"Then I'll do it myself!" said the little red hen. And she did.

The little red hen made the flour into dough by adding milk, eggs, and yeast. She kneaded the dough and let it rise. Then she kneaded the dough again and let it rise. Finally she put it in the oven to bake.

Wonderful smells wafted out from the oven, through the whole house, and into the yard. The pig got out of his mud puddle and followed the smell of baking bread into the kitchen. The dog roused himself from his nap and followed his nose to the kitchen. The cat sniffed the air, stretched, and then sashayed into the kitchen.

The little red hen took the bread from the oven.

"Who will help me eat this bread?" she asked.

"I will!" said the pig, who suddenly had nowhere to go.

"I will!" said the dog, who was no longer sleepy.

"I will!" said the cat, who licked her mouth in anticipation.

"No you won't!" declared the little red hen. "I found the grain of wheat. I planted and tended it. I harvested it. I took the wheat to the miller to be ground into flour. I made the dough and baked the bread. And I'm going to eat it all myself!"

And she did. After that, the pig, the dog, and the cat all did their part of the work around the house.

"C" STORIES, LONGER BUT NOT HARDER

The Frog Prince

A German tale retold by Annie Weissman

Once upon a time there was a princess who was beautiful and spoiled. That meant she got everything she wanted and more besides.

One day she went for a walk in the forest, carrying her favorite toy, a golden ball. She tossed it up in the air and caught it. She tossed it up in the air and caught it. She tossed high into the air and couldn't catch it. The ball fell into a muddy pond.

"Oh, boo-hoo-hoo!" she cried.

A nasty little frog poked his head out of the pond.

"Why are you crying so, princess?"

"My ball went into the pond, and I can't get it out," she whined.

"I could retrieve your ball," he said. "But what will you give me in return?"

"I will give you my crown. I will give you my pearls. I will give you my pretty dress."

"What need have I of a crown or pearls or a pretty dress? What I ask is that you promise to let me eat from your golden plate and sleep upon your pillow for three days in a row."

"Oh, yes, I promise!" said the princess.

The frog dove under the water for the golden ball. Meanwhile the princess thought to herself, "I'm going to get my ball back and not have to pay anything for it!"

The frog came up from the bottom of the pond with the golden ball in his mouth. He tossed it to the princess. She wiped it clean on her gown and ran back to the castle.

"Wait for me, princess! Wait for me!" called the frog. But she never heard a word.

That night, the princess and her father, the king, sat down for dinner. There was a knock at the door. They heard some singing:

"Open the door, my princess dear.

Open the door, for thy true love is here.

Remember the words that thou and I said,

By the muddy pond and the green woodshed."

"Go and see who's there," ordered the king.

The princess went to the door and opened it. She looked outside but saw no one. She returned to her seat at the dinner table.

"Who was at the door?" asked the king.

"No one," the princess replied.

There was another knock at the door. And then came some singing:

"Open the door, my princess dear.

Open the door, for thy true love is here.

Remember the words that thou and I said,

By the muddy pond and the green woodshed."

"Go and see who's there," ordered the king.

The princess opened the door. She looked all around. Then she looked down and saw the frog. She shut the door in his face.

"Who is at the door?" thundered the king.

"It's just a n-nasty little frog!" said the princess. "He got my ball from the muddy pond. I promised that he could eat from my golden plate and sleep upon my pillow for three days in a row, but I didn't think he'd actually come to the palace!"

"You must keep your promises," said the king. "Open the door and let the frog in."

The princess stomped across the floor and opened the door. The frog came in and flip-flopped across the tiles to the dining table. He hopped onto the table and onto the princess's golden plate, and he started to eat.

"Ee-you!" said the princess. "I'm not eating any more from that plate!"

When the frog was full, he stretched and said, "I'm tired Princess. Take me to your room."

The princess picked up the frog and held him by one foot, away from her body, as she climbed up the stairs to her room. Once inside, she went to a corner.

"No, no, Princess!" said the frog. "I must sleep upon your pillow."

"No you won't!" shouted the princess.

"I'll tell your father that you aren't keeping your promise," said the frog.

So the princess took her pillow and put it at the end of her bed. She went to sleep at the other end.

When she awoke the next morning, the frog was gone.

"I hope I never see that nasty frog again!" she said, and she promptly forgot all about him.

When the princess and the king sat down for dinner that night, there came a knock on the door and the singing.

> "Open the door, my princess dear.
> Open the door, for thy true love is here.
> Remember the words that thou and I said,
> By the muddy pond and the green woodshed."

"Open the door and let the frog in!" ordered the king.

The princess stomped across the floor and opened the door. The frog came in and flip-flopped across the tiles to the dining table. He hopped onto the table and onto the princess's golden plate, and he started to eat.

"Ee-you!" said the princess. "I'm not eating any more from that plate!"

When the frog was full, he stretched and said, "I'm tired Princess. Take me to your room."

The princess picked up the frog and held him by one foot, away from her body, as she climbed up the stairs to her room. Once inside, she went to a corner.

"No, no, Princess!" said the frog. "I must sleep upon your pillow."

"Hmmph!" said the princess as she took her pillow and put it at the end of her bed. She went to sleep at the other end.

When she awoke the next morning, the frog was gone.

"I hope I never see that nasty frog again!" she said. She ate a rather large lunch, just in case he came again that night.

When the princess and the king sat down for dinner that night, there came a knock on the door and the singing.

> "Open the door, my princess dear.
> Open the door, for thy true love is here.
> Remember the words that thou and I said,
> By the muddy pond and the green woodshed."

"Open the door and let the frog in!" ordered the king.

The princess stomped across the floor and opened the door. The frog came in and flip-flopped across the tiles to the dining table. He hopped onto the table and onto the princess's golden plate, and he started to eat.

"Ee-you!" said the princess. "I'm not eating any more from that plate!"

When the frog was full, he stretched.

"I know," said the princess, "you're tired."

She picked up the frog and held him by one foot, away from her body, as she climbed up the stairs to her room. Once inside, she didn't go to the corner. She took her pillow and put it at the end of her bed. She went to sleep at the other end.

When she awoke the next morning, the frog was gone. In his place was a handsome prince.

"Who are you?" she gasped.

"I was that nasty little frog," said the prince. "A spell was put upon me so that I would remain a frog until a real princess let me eat from her golden plate and sleep upon her pillow for three days in a row. You have broken the spell."

Their eyes met and they fell in love.

"Will you marry me?" asked the prince.

"Yes," said the princess.

So they sent word to the prince's castle that he was alive and where he was. His father sent a coach with eight fancy horses and a driver to fetch the prince.

The prince and princess went to his kingdom, were married, and lived happily ever after.

The Talking Yam

A folktale from Ghana retold by Annie Weissman

Once there lived a farmer who grew yams. When it was time to harvest the vegetables, he started to dig up his yams. As he uncovered one, it spoke to him.

"So now you've come around to dig us up and eat us. Where were you when we needed water? Where were you when we were being choked by weeds?"

The farmer thought he was alone and couldn't figure out who was talking.

"Did you moo?" he asked the cow.

"It was the yam talking," said his dog. "It said to leave it alone because you didn't weed and water it."

The farmer had never heard his dog talk before, and he didn't like the dog's attitude. He cut a small branch from a nearby tree to hit the dog.

"Put that branch down!" ordered the tree. "You hurt me by cutting it off me."

"Put me down gently!" demanded the branch.

The shocked farmer put the branch down on a rock.

"Take that branch off me!" complained the rock.

This was too much for the farmer. He was shocked, scared, and angry. He ran down the road toward the village. He met a fisherman who had just caught a large fish.

"Why are you running for your life?" asked the fisherman.

"I tried to dig my yams this morning, but one said that I hadn't weeded and watered it. My dog repeated what the yam said. When I cut a branch to hit him, the tree complained and told me to put down the branch. The branch said to put it down gently, so I did, on a rock. The rock said to take the branch off it."

"You have some imagination!" said the fisherman.

"Did you take the branch off the rock?" asked the fish on the end of the line.

"EEK!" yelled the fisherman. He threw down his fishing pole and ran down the road with the farmer.

They met a weaver with a bundle of cloth on his head.

"Why are you running?" he asked.

The farmer told his story of the talking yam, the talking dog, the talking tree, the talking branch, and the talking rock.

"And then," said the fisherman, "the fish I'd just caught wanted to know if the farmer had taken the branch off the rock!"

The weaver listened to their story, but didn't believe any of it.

"You two are scared for nothing!"

The weaver's bundle of cloth said, "If it happened to you, you'd be scared and run, too!"

"AAAHH!" yelled the weaver, and he joined the farmer and the fisherman running down the road.

They met a man bathing in the river.

"Is there some trouble?" he called out.

"I tried to dig my yams this morning," said the farmer, "but one said that I hadn't weeded and watered it. My dog repeated what the yam had said. When I cut a branch to hit him, the tree complained and told me to put down the branch. The branch said to put it down gently, so I did, on a rock. The rock said to take the branch off it."

"Then my fish asked if he took the branch off the stone!" said the fisherman.

"And my cloth said, 'You'd be scared, too, if it happened to you,'" said the weaver.

"What a bunch of silliness!" laughed the bather. "That's the best story I've heard in a long time."

"You wouldn't think it was silly if it happened to you!" said the water.

"Oh no!" cried the bather. He scrambled out of the water and into his clothes, and ran with the farmer, the fisherman, and the weaver.

When they reached the village, they went to see the chief. Many villagers followed to see what was going on.

The chief held up his hand to silence everyone. His servant brought his golden stool outside. The chief sat upon it.

"Why are you so upset?" demanded the chief.

"I tried to dig my yams this morning," said the farmer, "but one said that I hadn't weeded and watered it. My dog repeated what the yam had said. When I cut a branch to hit him, the tree complained and told me to put down the branch. The branch said to put it down gently, so I did, on a rock. The rock said to take the branch off it."

"Then my fish asked if he took the branch off the rock!" said the fisherman.

"And my cloth said, 'You'd be scared, too, if it happened to you,'" said the weaver.

"And the river said, 'You wouldn't think it was silly if it happened to you!'" said the bather.

The chief looked at the four men and shook his head.

"You talk so much that you don't make sense!" said the chief. "Go back to work and stop fooling around!"

The four men hung their heads and went back down the road. The villagers saw the show was over and went about their business.

"Huh!" said the golden stool. "What a story! Talking yams!"

The Gunniwolf

A German folktale retold by Annie Weissman

Once upon a time, a mother lived with her little girl at the edge of the forest. The mother always told the daughter not to go into the forest, for a gunniwolf lived there. He was large and hairy and scary. The mother told the little girl that if she should ever meet the gunniwolf, she should not move or the gunniwolf would harm her. She should sing a song because the gunniwolf loved to hear children sing.

One day, the mother had to go to the market, so she told the little girl to be sure to stay at home, locked in the house.

A little while after the mother had gone, the little girl was looking out the window. She saw some beautiful red and white flowers growing at the edge of the forest. She thought about how nice these flowers would look on the kitchen table. Forgetting all about her mother's instructions, the little girl went outside to pick the flowers. She saw even-more-beautiful flowers farther into the forest, so she ran to pick them. She went deeper and deeper into the forest without realizing it. As she picked the flowers, she sang:

> "Rock-a-bye, baby,
> In the treetop,
> When the wind blows,
> The cradle will rock."

All of a sudden, UP JUMPED THE GUNNIWOLF!

The little girl remembered that her mother had told her to stand still.

"Where are you going?" asked the gunniwolf gruffly.

"I'm not going anywhere," the little girl replied.

"Sing that sweet song again!" demanded the gunniwolf.

So the little girl sang this song:

> "Rock-a-bye, baby,
> In the treetop,
> When the wind blows,
> The cradle will rock."

The gunniwolf's eyes started to close. The little girl sang the song more softly.

> "When the wind blows,
> The cradle will fall ... "

The gunniwolf was asleep and snoring. The little girl started to run toward home. The sound of her feet was *pump, pump, pump.*

But the gunniwolf woke up and found the little girl gone. He ran after her, *boundie-down, boundie-down, boundie-down.*

Pump, pump, pump, boundie-down, boundie-down, boundie-down. The gunniwolf caught up to the little girl. She stopped and stood still.

"Why did you move?" growled the gunniwolf.

"I won't move," she said, crossing her fingers behind her back.

"Sing that sweet song to me again!" demanded the gunniwolf.

So the little girl sang the song.

> "Rock-a-bye, baby,
> In the treetop,
> When the wind blows,
> The cradle will rock."

The gunniwolf's eyes started to close. The little girl sang the song more softly.

> "When the wind blows,
> The cradle will fall ... "

The gunniwolf was asleep and snoring. The little girl started to run toward home. The sound of her feet was *pump, pump, pump.*

But the gunniwolf woke up and found the little girl gone. He ran after her, *boundie-down, boundie-down, boundie-down.*

Pump, pump, pump, boundie-down, boundie-down, boundie-down. The gunniwolf caught up to the little girl. She stopped and stood still.

"Why did you move?" growled the gunniwolf.

"I won't move," she said, crossing her fingers behind her back.

"Sing that sweet song to me again!" demanded the gunniwolf.

So the little girl sang the song.

> "Rock-a-bye, baby,
> In the treetop,
> When the wind blows,
> The cradle will rock."

The gunniwolf's eyes started to close. The little girl sang the song more softly.

> "When the wind blows,
> The cradle will fall ... "

The gunniwolf was asleep and snoring.

The little girl started to run toward home. The sound of her feet was *pump, pump, pump.* She saw her house. *Pump, pump, pump.* She ran inside the house and locked the doors. And she never went into the forest alone again.

Lazy Jack

An English folktale retold by Annie Weissman

Once a young man named Jack lived with his mother. In the summertime he would sit under the tall trees and drink cool lemonade. In the wintertime he would sit by the fireside and drink hot chocolate. He never worked.

One day his mother said, "Jack, I'm tired of doing all the work around here. I take in laundry and sewing so we can eat. If you don't get a job, you can't eat my food!"

The next day, Jack was hired out to a farmer. At the end of the day, the farmer gave Jack a penny. Jack had never had a penny before. He turned it over in his hand, watched it shine, and then flipped it from hand to hand. He was doing this as he crossed a river. He flipped the penny too far and it disappeared into the rushing water.

When he got home and told his mother what had happened, she said, "Lazy Jack, you are silly, you are slack. The next time, you put it in your pocket."

"Okay," said Jack, "I'll do that the next time."

The next day Jack was hired out to a dairy farmer. At the end of the day, the farmer gave Jack an open bottle of milk. Jack remembered what his mother had said, so he put that bottle of milk in his pants pocket, and he skipped and danced all the way home. By the time he got there, most of the milk had slopped out of the bottle onto his pants and the path. There was just a bit of milk left.

When he got home and told his mother what had happened, she said, "Lazy Jack, you are silly, you are slack. The next time you put it on your head and walk home slowly."

"Okay," said Jack, "I'll do that the next time."

The next day Jack was hired out to the very same dairy farmer. At the end of the day, the farmer gave him a big wad of butter. Jack remembered what his mother had said, so he balanced the butter on his head and walked home slowly. The butter melted on his face, down his neck, and onto his clothes. When he got home, he was a sticky mess.

He told his mother what had happened.

She said, "Lazy Jack, you are silly, you are slack. The next time you wrap it in cool leaves and hold it in front of you."

"Okay," said Jack, "I'll do that the next time."

The next day he was hired out to a baker. At the end of the day, the baker gave Jack an old tomcat. Jack remembered what his mother had said, so he wrapped the cat in cool leaves and held it in front of him. Cats don't like to be held like that. The cat scratched Jack, ripped his shirt, and ran away.

When he got home and told his mother what had happened, she said, "Lazy Jack, you are silly, you are slack. The next time you tie a string around it and drag it behind you."

"Okay," said Jack, "I'll do that the next time."

The next day Jack was hired by the butcher. At the end of the day, this generous man gave Jack a big ham. Jack remembered what his mother had said. He wrapped a string around the ham and dragged it behind him. All the dogs in town followed Jack and took big bites out of the ham. When they were done, the insects attacked it. When Jack got home there was nothing but a dirty, buggy, bone.

When he got home, he told his mother what had happened. She thought about the ham dinners they could have had and the soup she could have made from a clean bone. She almost cried.

"Lazy Jack, you are silly, you are slack! The next time you put it on your shoulder."

"Okay," said Jack, "I'll do that the next time."

The next day Jack was hired out to a rancher. At the end of the day, the rancher gave Jack a donkey. Now Jack remembered what his mother had said. It took him half an hour to hoist that donkey onto his shoulders.

In the town where Jack lived, there was a very rich man with a daughter named Esmerelda. She had never smiled or laughed. Her father said that whoever could make her laugh could live with them and share in their riches. No one had been able to make her laugh.

Esmerelda happened to be looking out the window as Jack staggered by, with the donkey on his shoulders. Her mouth started to twitch. It went into a smile. She started to laugh! She laughed and laughed until her father rushed in to find out what had finally made his daughter happy. She was laughing too hard to speak, but she pointed out the window. When the rich man saw Jack, with the donkey on his shoulders, he laughed. He ordered a servant to ask Jack to come in.

The servant told Jack that the rich man wanted to see him.

"Okay," said Jack, "but it took me half an hour to get this donkey on my shoulders. I'm not taking it off."

Jack struggled up the stairs, with the donkey on his shoulders. When he was shown into the parlor, the rich man asked him why he had a donkey on his shoulders. Jack told them the whole tale, starting with the penny.

The rich man and his daughter laughed so hard that tears ran down their faces and their sides ached.

"Jack, you have done what no one else could! You have brought joy and laughter to my daughter's life. You and your mother may live with us and share our wealth.

Jack went home and got his mother and they moved into the rich man's house.

Now, in the summertime Jack and Esmerelda sit under the tall trees and drink cool lemonade. In the wintertime they sit by the fireside and drink hot chocolate. And that's the story of a very lucky but lazy Jack.

Myths

A Greek myth retold by Annie Weissman

Pyramus and Thisbe

In Babylonia, there once lived a very handsome young man named Pyramus. Next door lived a very beautiful young woman name Thisbe. They fell in love and wanted to marry, but both sets of parents forbade it. The parents could forbid the marriage, but they could not forbid the love that grew deeper and deeper for both Pyramus and Thisbe. They communicated with signs and looks. The love smoldered even more because it was forbidden.

Pyramus and Thisbe discovered a crack in the wall between their houses. What joy! They could whisper all day long. When night came, each kissed a side of the wall.

One day, when they whispered through the crack in the wall, they decided to sneak out of their homes that night and go outside the city to a building called the Tomb of Ninus. They would meet at the foot of a particular white mulberry tree, near a stream.

Thisbe snuck away first, hiding her face under a veil. She reached the mulberry tree and sat down, alone, in the dim evening light. Suddenly, she saw a lioness, whose mouth was bloody from eating her dinner. The lioness was drinking at the stream. Thisbe ran farther down the path and hid behind a rock. In her hurry, she dropped her veil.

After the lioness finished her drink, she saw the veil, took it in her mouth, and played with it. The veil got blood all over it. When the lioness got tired of playing, she left the bloody veil and returned to the woods.

Pyramus arrived a little later at the meeting place. He saw the tracks of the lioness, and then he found the bloody veil.

"Oh, Thisbe!" he wailed. "I am the cause of your death! I tempted you into danger and wasn't here to protect you. You are more worthy to live than me! Come, lion, and tear me apart!"

Pyramus took the veil to the white mulberry tree, the place where they were supposed to meet. He covered the veil with his kisses and his tears.

"My blood will join yours on this veil," he said. He drew his sword and plunged it into his own heart. Blood spurted from his wound, turning some of the white mulberries red, and soaking the ground. The tree's roots absorbed Pyramus's blood and sent it all through the tree, turning all the white mulberries red.

Meanwhile, Thisbe timidly came out of her hiding place, not wanting to miss Pyramus. She was eager to tell him of the danger she had escaped. When she came to the mulberry tree, she saw the red berries. She thought she was at the wrong meeting place. As she hesitated, she saw someone on the ground. She recognized Pyramus and ran to him. She realized he was dying. She cried tears into his wound and kissed his cold lips.

"Pyramus! It is I, your Thisbe! Who has done this to you?"

When Pyramus heard Thisbe's name, he opened his eyes once, looked at her, and died.

Thisbe saw her blood-stained veil and his own scabbard, empty of his sword.

"You killed yourself over grief for me!" she said. "I can be brave. My love is as strong as yours. We couldn't be together in life, but we can be together in death. Let us be buried in one tomb. Let the berries of this tree remain red, as a memorial to our love."

The parents buried both Pyramus and Thisbe in one tomb. And the mulberry tree has reddish-purple berries to this day.

Pygmalion

A Roman myth retold by Annie Weissman

In Cyprus, there lived a man named Pygmalion. He saw many faults in women and so grew to hate women. He decided that he would never marry. Pygmalion was a sculptor. He took a piece of ivory and used his great skill to make a woman more beautiful than any living woman. The statue was so beautiful that it seemed alive, just too shy to move.

Pygmalion admired his statue, his own work, so much that he fell in love with it. He had to touch it to convince himself that she was not alive, and still, sometimes, he couldn't believe it was only ivory. He caressed the statue and gave it presents that he would have given a real young woman: shells and polished stones, little birds, and colorful flowers. He made the ivory woman fine clothing and gave her sparkling jewelry. He hung earrings from her ears and pearls around her neck. She looked even more beautiful after he dressed her up. He laid her on a couch with embroidered upholstery, put a feathered pillow under her head as if she could feel its softness, and called her his wife.

Soon came the festival of Venus, the goddess of love and beauty. Pygmalion burned incense at the altar and asked the gods to give him a wife like his ivory statue. He was too shy to ask for his ivory statue to come to life. Venus heard him and knew what he really wanted. She sent a sign by making the fire at the altar flame up three times.

When Pygmalion went home, he leaned down to the couch and kissed his ivory statue. The lips felt warm. He kissed her again and touched her arm. The ivory felt soft. He stood up, astonished. He thanked Venus, and then leaned down and kissed the ivory statue again. It was a statue no longer. The woman felt his kisses and blushed. She opened her eyes shyly and looked at Pygmalion. They were married with Venus's blessings.

Web Sites

National Council of Teachers of English, National
    Language Arts Standards
<http://www.ncte.org/standards>

Arizona Department of Education's Language Arts Standards
<http://www.ade.az.gov/standards>

New York State English Language Arts Standards
<http://www.emsc.nysed.gov/ciai/ela/elastandards/
    elamap.html>

Aesop's and La Fontaine's Fables
<http://www.AesopFables.com>

Paul Bunyan Stories
<http://www.newnorth.net/~bmorren/bunyan.html>

Stories about Annie Christmas, Pecos Bill, Paul Bunyan,
    Casey Jones, and Mike Fink
<http://www.thinkquest.org/library/lib/site_sum_
    outside.html?tname=J001779&turl=J001779/
    stories1.htm>

Kids' Storytelling Club
<http://www.storycraft.com/files/welcome.htm>

The National Storytelling Network (with links to the
    Youth Olympics)
<http://www.storynet.org>

Voices Across America Youth Storytelling
<http://members.cnetech.com/kctells>

Storytelling in the Classroom
<http://www.storyarts.org/classroom>

Directories of Storytellers
<http://www.eduscapes.com/42explore/story.htm>
<http://www.storyteller.net>

The Eighth Annual Storytelling Festival at Westwood
    Middle School
<http://www.sbac.edu/~talbot/JCF_story.html>

OTHER STORYTELLING WEB SITES

Storytelling Magazine
<http://www.storynet.org/Magazine/mag.htm>

The Kennedy Center African Odyssey
<http://artsedge.kennedy-center.org/aoi/opps/spin/
    storyart3.html>

Storytelling, Drama, and Creative Arts
<http://falcon.jmu.edu/~ramseyil/drama.htm>

Aaron Shepard's Storytelling Page
<http://www.aaronshep.com/storytelling/>

Tim Sheppard's Storytelling Resources
<http://www.timsheppard.co.uk/story/>

The Art of Storytelling
<http://www.seanet.com/~eldrbarry/roos/art.htm>

Handbook for Storytellers
<http://falcon.jmu.edu/~ramseyil/storyhandbook.htm>

General Bibliography of Works on Storytelling

Baker, Augusta, and Ellin Greene. *Storytelling Art &
Technique*. New York: Bowker, 1987.

Bauer, Caroline Feller. *The New Handbook for Storytellers*.
Bauer: ALA, 1993.

Bettleheim, Bruno. *Uses of Enchantment: The Meaning and
Importance of Fairy Tales*. New York: Knopf, 1976.

Birch, Carol L., and Melissa A. Heckler. *Who Says? Essays
on Pivotal Issues in Contemporary Storytelling*.
Little Rock, AR: August, 1996.

Breneman, Lucille N., and Bren Breneman. *Once Upon a
Time: A Storytelling Handbook*. Chicago: Nelson, 1983.

Byrd, Susannah Mississippi. *Using a Bilingual Storybook
in the Classroom: A Teacher's Guide to Tell Me a
Cuento/Cuentame un story*. El Paso, TX: Cinco
Puntos, 1998.

Cassady, Marsh. *The Art of Storytelling: Creative Ideas for
Preparation and Performance*. Colorado Springs,
CO: Meriwether, 1994.

Colum, Padraic. *Story Telling Old and New*. 1927. New
York: Macmillan, 1968.

Lipman, Doug. *Improving Your Storytelling*. Little Rock,
AR: August, 1997.

Livo, Norma J., and Sandra A. Reitz. *Storytelling: Process
and Practice*. Englewood Cliffs, NJ: Libraries
Unlimited, 1986.

MacDonald, Margaret Read. *The Storytellers Start-Up
Book: Finding, Learning, Performing & Using
Folktales Including Twelve Tellable Tales*. Little
Rock, AR: August, 1993.

Marsh, Valerie. *Storyteller's Sampler*. Fort Atkinson, WI:
Alleyside, 1996.

Mooney, Bill, and David Holt. *The Storyteller's Guide*.
Little Rock, AR: August, 1996.

National Storytelling Association, *Tales as Tools: The
Power of Story in the Classroom*. Jonesboro, TN:
National Storytelling, 1994.

Pellowski, Anne. *The Storytelling Handbook*. New York:
Simon, 1995.

—. *The World of Storytelling*. New York: Bowker, 1977.

Shedlock, Marie L. *The Art of the Storyteller*. 1915. New
York: Dover, 1951.

Shelley, Marshall. *Telling Stories to Children*. Batavia, IL:
Lion, 1990.

Webber, Desiree Corn, et al. *Travel the Globe:
Multicultural Story Times*. Englewood, CO:
Libraries Unlimited, 1998.

Weissman, Annie. *Transforming Storytimes into Reading and
Writing Lessons*. Worthington, OH: Linworth, 2001.

Alphabetical List of Stories

About the Author

Annie Weissman has been working with libraries, schools, books, and children for many years and in many capacities. She has been a high school teacher, a children's librarian, an elementary school librarian, a faculty associate in library science at Arizona State University, a principal, a supervisor of student teachers at ASU West, a public speaker, and an author. A past recipient of The Progressive Library Media Award and the Excellence in Education Award, she is currently active in leadership positions in the Arizona Library Association. The author resides in Phoenix, Arizona.